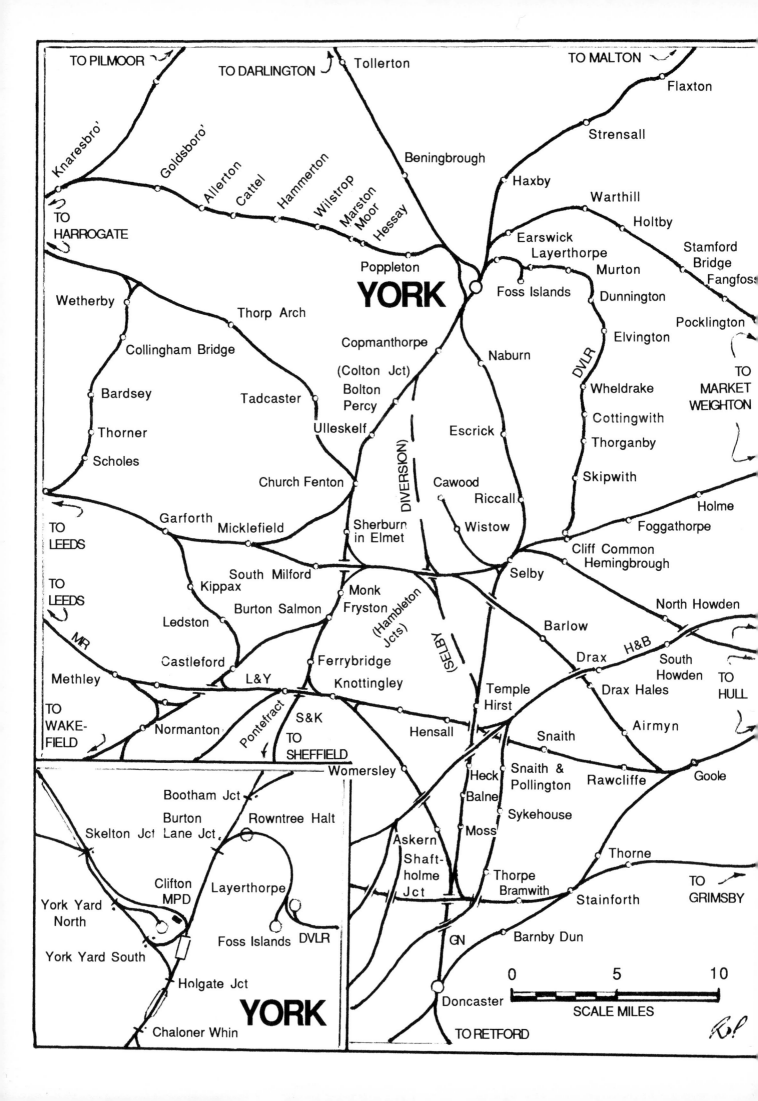

BRITAIN'S RAIL SUPER CENTRES

YORK

BRITAIN'S RAIL SUPER CENTRES

YORK

KEN APPLEBY

Ian Allan Publishing

First published 1993

ISBN 0 7110 2072 8

Published by Ian Allan Ltd, Shepperton, Surrey; and printed by Ian Allan Printing Ltd at their works at Coombelands in Runnymede, England.

Previous page:
Raven Pacific locomotive No 2402 was named *City of York*. **Here the locomotive is pictured in pristine ex-Darlington Works condition in March 1924.** *BR*

Front and rear endpapers: **Railways around York.** *R. D. Pulleyn*

Contents

Preface

Ten years ago I contributed a foreword to the late Ken Hoole's book entitled Rail Centres: York, and, but for the author's untimely death on 27 December 1988, it is more than likely that he, rather than I, would have been called upon to write this latest version, which brings the York railway story right up to date. A lot has happened on the railway scene in and around York since the original book was published in 1983, and because I regard it as something of an honour to have been invited to follow in Ken Hoole's literary footsteps, this work is dedicated to the memory of the man who, in my opinion, was the doyen of North Eastern Railway historians.

The ancient city of York – Eboracum to the Romans and Jorvik to the Vikings – has a long, eventful and distinguished history which goes back almost 2,000 years, and whilst its railways only appeared on the scene less than 200 years ago, their story is particularly worthy of being told. We have come a long way from the days of George Hudson – perhaps better remembered as 'The Railway King' – whose drive and initiative, combined with unorthodox and unethical (even dubious!) business methods did much to ensure that York well and truly secured a strategic place in the expanding railway network of the day. Indeed, at one time, there was even a distinct possibility that York could have finished up at the end of a branch line from Leeds – but Hudson soon squashed that idea!

Nevertheless, as the system grew during the 1840s even the Hudson empire was swallowed up in a succession of amalgamations out of which emerged the North Eastern Railway in 1854. This benevolent monopoly served a large territory situated between the rivers Humber and Tweed, and became one of the most progressively influential and financially strong railway companies –

despite the lack of its own London terminus!

The old North Eastern certainly liked to do things on a grand scale, and the present York station, which dates from 1877, proudly stands as a memorial both to this great company and to our Victorian forebears who boldly designed and engineered it.

Railways first came to York in 1839, and the unfolding story of their development up to the present day has a particular fascination. There are many varied facets of the railway scene to be observed at York. Here, for example, one can still see impressive buildings which originally formed part of the 1841 'old station', and pause for a while to admire the architectural merits of the 1906 Headquarters Offices, which housed the North Eastern's managerial and administrative heart. Then there is the 1877 station with its magnificent curved roof, where all the latest and most sophisticated hardware of a busy modern railway can be seen in action against a 19th century backcloth. Nor has York forgotten its links with the earlier railways from which the present system evolved. Here at the National Railway Museum one can find a combination of things both ancient and modern. Thus, not only is there much to be seen of our rich railway heritage, but also the evolution of railway transport right up to the present day can be comprehensively traced.

The expansion, change and subsequent decline of a once extensive network of marshalling yards, sidings, locomotive sheds and workshops form yet another part of the York railway story. Furthermore, we have moved right through the steam and diesel era up to the InterCity 225 electrics; from basic carriages (with foot-warmers as an optional extra!) to the standards of luxury on wheels we now accept as commonplace, and from primitive train sig-

nalling methods to the very latest in computerised technology. So, York has all the essentials of a thriving modern railway centre where there is always something of interest to be seen.

Since Ken Hoole's book appeared in 1983, many of the projected changes mentioned therein have since taken place. For instance, a stretch of the 1871 main line south of York going towards Selby has been superseded by a completely new railway which avoids the Selby coalfield; and main line electrification, so strongly advocated by Sir Vincent Raven – the North Eastern's last Chief Mechanical Engineer – well over 70 years ago, was finally achieved during 1991.

Throughout this book, much emphasis has been placed upon what might be termed 'modern history'. Yet comparatively recent happenings, even today's news, soon becomes tomorrow's history – hence all the more reason why such events need to be chronicled in some detail before time passes by and memories fade.

In this respect I make no apology for having expanded the narrative to include much of the territory now controlled by York's new 'high-tech' signal box – or Integrated Electronic Control Centre (IECC) to call it by its proper name! – hence reference is made, purely in the context of ECML infrastructure changes and resignalling, to places outside York such as Selby, Thirsk and Northallerton – even the Redmire branch!

York was, still is, and hopefully will continue to be a railway centre of great importance and interest – truly a 'Rail Super Centre' in every sense! This work, therefore, seeks to portray an ongoing saga of change and development since the modest beginnings back in 1839. Long may York and its railways prosper!

K. C. Appleby   York
October 1992

The high-tech way of fixing rail fastenings. A Permaclipper at work on the Selby diversion. *BR*

Acknowledgements

A work of this nature could not have been successfully undertaken without the co-operation which was so generously forthcoming from a wide variety of sources – particularly in the case of research facilities and the provision of photographs. Both British Rail and the National Railway Museum were extremely helpful in this respect. Similarly, a number of my former railway colleagues, together with many friends in various railway historical societies, have all made their contribution.

Especial thanks are due to David Thompson, Keith Metcalfe and Robert Anderson of British Rail for the use of photographs. Also, I am indebted to certain railway colleagues regarding their patience and forebearance following my retirement from BR – especially Peter Armstrong, Dennis Coward, Trefor Davies, Derek Davies and Chris Jacob. Rob Shorland-Ball and many of the NRM staff, particularly Christine Heap and Jane Elliott, must also be thanked for their help – nothing has been too much trouble.

Two of my friends – both members of the Signalling Record Society *and* the North Eastern Railway Association – John Boyes and Richard Pulleyn, deserve a mention for the contributions they have made towards this work, particularly Richard Pulleyn's excellent drawings.

Also, it has to be said that my family have helped this project along in their different ways. Some of the credit belongs to my late wife, Muriel, who initially offered much encouragement and inspiration during the early stages of research – but sadly did not live long enough to see the finished work. My daughter, Sue Fraser, and her husband Paul, gave me the use of their word processor and undertook the task of editing the manuscript. My daughter in law, Catrina Appleby, photographed some of the modern scenes which appear herein, and my son Geoff kept me right up to date regarding the 'present day' railway.

Finally, I must thank my publishers for allowing me to 'raid' their photographic library.

KCA

1. Outline History - The 1830s Onwards

A complete and detailed history of York's early railways, together with the part played by the famous (or infamous) George Hudson in their development, could almost demand a whole volume being written in its own right. However, such a book would doubtless prove to be somewhat tedious, even rather boring, hence it seems preferable to present a reasonably concise historical summary in order to highlight the most significant events. For centuries York has been a major centre of transport and communications. Even the Romans recognised it as a strategic location, important enough to justify the establishment of a garrison city in 71 AD called Eboracum.

Water transport along the River Ouse also played a part in York's development, as did the eventual growth of a stage-coach network which necessitated the provision of numerous coaching inns. Nor must one overlook the significance of York as an ecclesiastical centre, for the sheer magnificence of its famous cathedral – better known as York Minster – frequently appears in the background of many a railway photograph.

The coming of the railway in 1839, and the subsequent expansion of what then represented a completely new mode of transport marked the start of a close association between the city and its railways, which has lasted right up to the present day. York has successively been the headquarters of the York & North Midland Railway (1839-1854), the North Eastern Railway (1854-1922), the London & North Eastern Railway – North Eastern Area (1923-1947), the North Eastern Region of British Rail-

Right:
George Hudson – 'The Railway King'. A lithograph by George Raphael Ward of an original painting by Sir Francis Grant RA for the Wear Commissioners' office in Sunderland, and now on exhibition at the Monkwearmouth Railway Station Museum. *BR*

Above:
The site of the temporary Y&NM station outside the city walls, in use from 29 May 1839 to 4 January 1841, photographed in 1939 to mark the centenary of the line's opening. The south end of the 1877 station can be seen to the left, with the wall of the former No 1 Erecting Shop of the Locomotive Works to the right. Across the centre of the photograph is Queen Street bridge, with the city walls in the background. The semaphore signal protected a level crossing which gave access to the Signal Engineers Stores (now disused) situated just within the walls. *BR*

ways (1948-1967), and finally the enlarged Eastern Region following its merger with the former North Eastern Region in 1967. Indeed, as the headquarters' location of the earliest railways and their successors, railwaymen over the years have played a large part in the civic life of the city, many of them attaining the highest offices of Lord Mayor and Sheriff.

The George Hudson Influence

The early history of York's railways tends to be dominated by George Hudson (1800-1871) – 'The Railway King' – whose initial enterprise, the York & North Midland of 1839, soon became part of a fast growing railway network constructed during the 1840s – a period often referred to as the 'Railway Mania'. Many of the early lines in northeastern England owed their inception and growth to the 'Hudson Influence'. George Hudson was born on 10 March 1800 at Howsham, a village in the old East Riding of Yorkshire situated not far from Stamford Bridge. He came to York in 1815 to be apprenticed to Nicholson & Bell, a firm of drapers and silk mercers, and in 1821 married Elizabeth Nicholson, the daughter of one of the partners. In 1827 he inherited the sum of £30,000 (a fortune in those days!) from his great uncle, and with his new-found wealth entered political life as a Tory (York was a Whig – or Liberal to use present day language – city in those days), becoming Lord Mayor of York three times in 1837,

1838 and 1846 respectively. He was also a Member of Parliament (for Sunderland) from 1845, and acquired a reputation for what might now be termed 'wheeling and dealing'. Furthermore, his liking for civic ostentation and 'junketing' became almost legendary during his terms of office as Lord Mayor.

Hudson's involvement with railways went back to the initial meeting in 1833 which discussed a proposed line to serve the city with the avowed objective to cheapen the price of coal. By the early 1830s, the Stockton & Darlington Railway of 1825 was already well established and in 1830 the first major railway route to link two important cities, namely the Liverpool & Manchester had opened for business. Nearer to York, the Leeds & Selby Railway had opened in 1834 and in 1835 a company called the North Midland Railway was formed to build a line from Derby to Leeds.

The significance of these early railway developments was not lost upon George Hudson, and on 13 October 1835, following a meeting held in the Guildhall at York, the York & North Midland Railway was promoted with the stated objective of building a line from York to Normanton in order to connect with the North Midland line and thus form a route to the south (with London as the ultimate goal). Hudson became the Chairman of York's first railway company and within a decade his influence had extended far and wide as this new form of transport rapidly developed.

Inevitably, Hudson's unethical financial dealings and often unorthodox – even dubious – business methods caught up with him (methods which nowadays might have been called 'insider dealing'!) and led to his eventual downfall in 1849. Publicly disgraced (for things which under present day legislation would in all probability have merited a stiff prison sentence), Hudson disappeared from both railway and political life. He died in London on 14 December 1871 and was buried at Scrayingham (adjacent to his native village of Howsham) on 21 December 1871.

Hudson is credited with once having said something to the effect of 'make all the railways come to York', though no proof exists to support this popular legend. He did not make all the railways come to York; indeed, he actively discouraged the London & York Railway (later to become known as the Great Northern) from so doing, but despite his financial and business misdemeanours he must at least take some credit for bringing influence to bear which resulted in York becoming a major and strategically placed railway centre. Notwithstanding his faults, he was ahead of the crowd and in many ways he laid the foundations upon which the North Eastern Railway in later years could build and achieve its pre-eminence.

The York & North Midland Railway received its Act on 21 June 1836 authorising construction of a line from York to join the North Midland at Altofts Junction, 3/4 mile north of Normanton, together with a branch from Whitwood Junction (near Castleford) to Methley in order to give access over the North Midland to Leeds (at that time Hunslet Lane), plus curves to link up with the Leeds & Selby near Milford and an extension to reach the River Ouse at York. Southwards from Normanton , the North Midland afforded access to London (Euston Square) over the Midland Counties line (Derby-Leicester-Rugby), or the Derby-Birmingham and Birmingham-London routes. Incidentally, the North Midland, Midland Counties and Derby-Birmingham companies amalgamated in 1844 to form the Midland Railway under the Chairmanship of George Hudson. York's first railway was formally opened on 29 May 1839 and it ran from a temporary station situated just outside the city walls (in what is now part of York station car park) to a junction with the Leeds & Selby line at a place now known as Gascoigne Wood. A further stage followed on 11 May 1840 from a location now known as Sherburn Junction to Burton Salmon, with final completion through to Altofts Junction taking place on 1 July 1840 concurrently with the North Midland opening the remainder of their line between Rotherham (Masborough) and Leeds (Hunslet Lane).

The second railway to reach York was the Great North of England which approached the city from the north. Originally the GNE had obtained an Act to build a line from Gateshead to Croft (just south of Darlington) as part of a scheme for a railway from Gateshead to York. The Act for the section southwards from Croft received the Royal Assent in July 1837, though at this point the GNE seemed to have had a change of mind and planned to make for Tadcaster rather than York, doubtless with the aim of heading towards Leeds, and it needed a lot of persuasion by the Y&NM Directors to bring the projected line to York. In fact, in September 1836 the Chairman (George Hudson) and Directors of the Y&NM accompanied by the Lord Mayor of York held a meeting with the GNE Directors to 'remonstrate with them respecting their intention of taking their line south by way of Tadcaster, in preference to this city'. The Y&NM even went so far as to initiate a survey of their own from York to Croft so as to be in a position to oppose the GNE Bill if it persisted in by-passing York. In the event, the GNE decided it would be more prudent to make for York and by September 1837 the company was inviting tenders. Thus railways were soon under construction simultaneously both north and south of York – with the Y&NM having a few months lead and less distance to cover.

Although the Y&NM consulting engineer, George Stephenson, had recommended that the terminus at York should be built outside the city walls, the 1836 Act allowed the line to 'commence at or near a certain garden or parcel of land' within the walls to the north of a road now called Tanner Row, where much of the site was already occupied. Indeed, it was not until August 1838 that the Y&NM decided to build its station on this site providing that it could be purchased at a reasonable price, though slow progress with the negotiations soon prompted the decision to erect a temporary station situated outside the city walls in readiness for opening the following year (while George Hudson was still Lord Mayor). In the meantime, the Y&NM had been in negotiations with the GNE regarding a joint station for use by both companies, and following a meeting at Thirsk on 4 December 1838 a formal agreement between them was signed. To reach the station it was necessary to make an archway through the city walls (imagine trying to get planning permission for something like this nowadays!), and by July 1839 this aspect of the work had been completed.

The station (which we now know as the 'old station') was opened for Y&NM passenger traffic on 4 January 1841, but although the GNE commenced working goods traffic on the same day, its passenger trains did not start running to and from York until 30 March 1841. Nevertheless, with the opening of the GNE, a through route became available between Darlington and London (Euston Square), involving, of course, a reversal in the terminal station at York, and within the space of a few more years the 'Hudson influence' resulted in the railway system being extended through the counties of Durham and Northumberland to link up with the North British at Berwick-upon-Tweed and thus give access to Edinburgh.

York's third railway ran to Scarborough and it was ready for opening on 7 July 1845 with a special train conveying George Hudson and his guests. The public opening took place on the following day, and at the same time a branch from Rillington (east of Malton) to Pickering was opened to connect with the much earlier horse-drawn Whitby & Pickering Railway dating from 1836. The next line radiating from York to open was the Y&NM's Market Weighton branch which diverged from the Scarborough railway at Bootham Junction (located adjacent to Wigginton Road level crossing). Opened as far as Market Weighton on 4 October 1847, another 18 years was to elapse before the extension onwards to Beverley came into being on 1 May 1865. Next came the East & West Yorkshire Junction Railway from Poppleton Junction (now called Skelton Junction) to the outskirts of Knaresborough, which opened on 30 October 1848. It took another three years for this line to actually reach Knaresborough; it was extended to Starbeck on 1 October 1851 (and subsequently to Harrogate from 1 August 1862).

By 1848 a network of five railways radiated from York, although later developments occurred which modified certain routes as will be seen in subsequent chapters. However, by 1848 the Great Northern Railway – originally projected as the London & York – was pushing northwards and Hudson saw the monopoly of York-London traffic via his Midland Railway threatened. It will be recalled that Hudson strongly opposed

Below:
The same site on 6 August 1992. It now forms part of York station car park. Note Hudson House in the background.
Mrs C. A. Appleby

this line as one railway he did not want to come to York. But, when the writing was on the wall, he made a shrewd move and was instrumental in the Y&NM building a short stretch of line from Burton Salmon to Knottingley in order to link up with the Wakefield, Pontefract & Goole line (of the then newly formed Lancashire & Yorkshire Railway) which had opened on 1 April 1848. Around this time the L&Y was busy constructing a branch from Knottingley towards Askern to join up with the GN at what has sometimes been described as 'A ploughed field north of Doncaster'. (Actually the GN and L&Y met each other on the present day Askern branch a short distance north of the location now known as Shaftholme Junction). Thus Hudson's link line between Burton Salmon and Knottingley was destined to become part of an East Coast route from London to the north. However, the GN, seeing an easy way out of building some 25 miles of new railway northwards, decided to forego its aspirations for independent access to York and

settled instead for running powers over the L&Y and Y&NM which became effective from 8 August 1850.

The Knottingley-Askern line opened on 6 June 1848 and following completion of the GN route south of Peterborough it became possible to reach a temporary London terminus at Maiden Lane (via Retford, Lincoln and Boston of all places). Completion of the so-called 'Towns Line' between Peterborough, Grantham and Retford and the opening of London King's Cross station on 14 October 1852 were without doubt significant events in the development of York as a strategic railway centre, and by this time the East Coast route began to assume something like a recognisable shape. Another short piece of line opened during the 1840s was the curve between Holgate Bridge Junction and North Junction (which is better known by its present name of York Yard South). A precise date of opening seems to have eluded even the most eminent of North Eastern historians, for neither Tomlinson nor

Hoole have been able to pin this down to anything other than some time in 1846.

Finally, mention should be made of the ill-fated Y&NM direct line from Copmanthorpe to Leeds via Tadcaster authorised in 1846 but never completed, being overtaken by the events leading to Hudson's downfall in 1849. Nonetheless, a magnificent stone viaduct was built over the River Wharfe at Tadcaster which stands to the present day as a lasting memorial to the 'Railway King'. Whilst the viaduct never carried the intended train services between York and Leeds, it is of interest to note that a siding line was laid across it to serve a mill situated on the east bank of the Wharfe and remained in use well into the 1950s.

1854 – Enter the North Eastern Railway

The North Eastern Railway in its final form was fourth in size of the pre-Grouping companies; it served an area which extended from the Humber to the Tweed, and even crossed the Pennines to reach its western outposts at Tebay, Penrith and Carlisle. This great company started life on 31 July 1854, and originally it was formed by an amalgamation of three fairly important lines together with a small one. Two of these constituent companies served York; namely George Hudson's York & North Midland (Y&NM), and the York, Newcastle & Berwick (Y&NB) – which had started off as the Great North of England, subsequently was the York & Newcastle of 1846, and finally the Y&NB of 1847. The other main constituent was the Leeds Northern, (originally Leeds & Thirsk until 1851), which ran from Leeds via Harrogate, Ripon, Northallerton and Yarm to Stockton. The relatively insignificant Malton & Driffield (opened 1853) made up the number. By a process of further amalgamations and acquisitions, notably the Newcastle & Carlisle in 1862, the Stockton & Darlington in 1863 and the Blyth & Tyne in 1874, together with a number of smaller companies, the North Eastern expanded and went from strength to strength during the second half of the 19th century. It established a virtual monopoly throughout the territory it served – apart from competition subsequently engendered by the Hull & Barnsley Railway of 1885.

As the volume of traffic grew over what was soon to be regarded as the East Coast Main Line, the disavantages of a dead-end station became only too obvious to the newly formed NER. Furthermore, the existing route between Doncaster and York was becoming extremely inconvenient, relying as it did upon running powers over the Askern-Knottingley branch of the L&Y Railway. Another

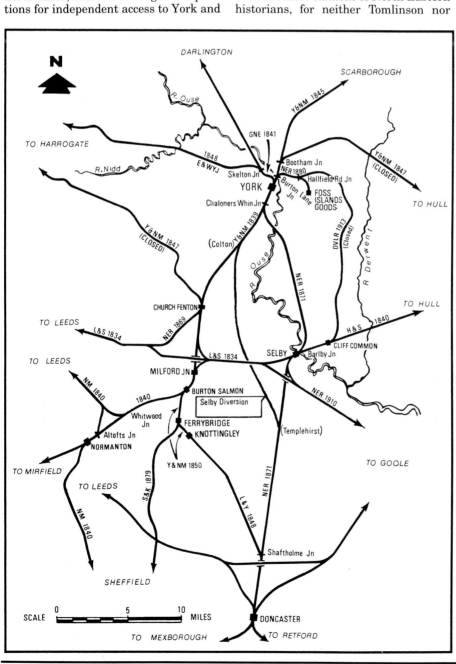

Left:
Map of the area surrounding York showing owning companies and date of opening.

problem associated with the 1841 station was that in order to gain access to and from the Scarborough direction, trains had to be drawn out to North Junction (now known as York Yard South) and vice-versa, thus the somewhat cramped and awkward terminal layout gave rise to much congestion and delay. During 1863 the NER applied for powers to construct two new stretches of line extending from what was later to be known as Chaloner Whin Junction (some two miles south of York) to Barlby Junction (north of Selby), and from Selby southwards to join the Great Northern (GN) at a location now called Shaftholme Junction. (The original course of the 1840 Hull-Selby route through Selby itself thus became part of the proposed main line.) The new line was opened on 2 January 1871, though trains still had to use the old station at York.

By 1865 parliamentary powers were being sought for a through station in York, to be situated outside the city walls, where the operating conditions would be greatly improved by avoidance of the need to work main line trains in and out of a terminus. The Act for a new station was obtained on 23 July 1866; but 11 years were to elapse before the scheme actually came to fruition.

Also included in the Act were powers to construct two new stretches of line; one from a junction near Holgate Bridge curving through the site of the new station to rejoin eventually the original GNE formation to the north, and the other being a short spur to join the north end of the new station to the Scarborough line. The new station finally opened on 25 June 1877, and concurrently with the passenger traffic being transferred from the old station, the former GNE line from North Junction (now York Yard South) was abandoned as part of it ran across the site. Although contemporary sources suggest that the route through the new station joined the old GNE line at Severus Junction (now York Yard North), there is no evidence to support the assumed construction of a physical junction at this point. Thus the new tracks must have been laid alongside the existing formation until they actually joined at Poppleton (now Skelton) Junction.

The railway map of York was by now virtually complete following the 1877 alterations. All that remained was the construction of the Foss Islands branch for which an Act had been obtained in 1874, and whilst a contract was let in 1877, the line from a junction with the Scarborough branch at Burton Lane to Foss Islands freight depot was not officially opened until 1 January 1880.

Apart from various extensions and alterations to track layouts, and provision of additional facilities as the volume of traffic – both passenger and freight – expanded, the Foss Islands branch was the last new railway in York to be built

Above:
A London & North Eastern Railway poster of the 1930s. *BR*

by the NER. (Actually the Derwent Valley built the most recent railway in York which opened in 1913, and ran from Layerthorpe Station to Cliff Common near Selby.)

The North Eastern Railway eventually absorbed the sole competitor within its midst, the Hull & Barnsley, from 1 April 1922 as a prelude to the Grouping which became effective on 1 January 1923. Arising out of the 1921 Railways Act, the various railway companies were formed into four main groups. Thus in 1923 the North Eastern, along with five other concerns (ie: the Great Northern, Great Central, Great Eastern, North British and Great North of Scotland), became part of the London & North Eastern Railway (LNER). Not only did the name 'North Eastern' continue in the new company's title, but also much of the LNER's organisation was devolved into three Areas, one of which – the North Eastern Area – continued to have its Headquarters at York thus maintaining the North Eastern tradition. Then to take things forward to more recent times, the railways were Nationalised following the 1947 Transport Act, and the LNER, along with the other three major railway companies (the LMSR, GWR and SR), became British Railways on 1 January 1948. Once again, the name survived upon the formation of a North Eastern Region within the BR organisational structure, but following the merger with the Eastern Region – effective from 1 January 1967 – the name 'North Eastern', after a period of 113 years, lost its unique identity.

Below:
The impressive NER headquarters building viewed from the city walls on 6 August 1992. Built to the basic structural design of William Bell (Chief Architect to the NER), and a consultant architect, Horace Field, who was engaged to design the exterior embellishments and interior detail, the offices were formally opened on 24 November 1906. The buildings still serve their original purpose – despite numerous reorganisations which have taken place over the years. The building to the right is the end of the former Royal Station Hotel, now part of the West Offices complex, and in the background is 37 Tanner Row, which was once the North Eastern Hotel.
Mrs C. A. Appleby

2. York's Passenger Stations - Old and New

The 'Old' Station

Contemporary accounts relate how York's very first passenger station was a somewhat basic structure, of wooden construction, located just outside the city walls; it was to be found within part of what now is the station car park near to the present Queen Street overbridge. Although good progress was being made with building the York & North Midland line itself, protracted negotiations concerning the acquisition of land for the construction of the proposed terminal station situated within the city walls produced an unacceptable delay, and it was decided in November 1838 that temporary facilities must be provided to enable the railway to be opened as planned on 29 May 1839. Hence a makeshift structure was erected which remained in use until the permanent station opened on 4 January 1841.

By 13 July 1839 work was completed on the first (northernmost) of the two archways which breached the city walls, thus permitting rails to be laid leading to temporary coal discharge facilities adjacent to the River Ouse near Tanners Moat, and during September 1839 preparatory work began on site clearance for construction of the permanent station. Originally Y&NM inspired, it was intended that the station would be

Above right:
An undated photograph looking through the 1839 'archway' towards the 'old' station. It was probably taken in the 1930s, judging from the types of vehicle on show. *Author's Collection*

Right:
The original Andrews' 'archway', which breached the city walls in 1839, looking towards the old station site on 6 August 1992. Note Hudson House in the background. The photographer was standing in the position formerly occupied by Archway Junction where the Y&NM and GNE lines converged.
Mrs C. A. Appleby

Above:
A drawing of the 1841 station, probably by the architect G. T. Andrews, purchased by the Friends of the NRM some 10 years ago and presented to the Museum. The office block was subsequently extended at each end and an additional storey added. *Crown Copyright; NRM, York*

Left:
Exterior view of the 1841 station frontage on to Tanner Row pictured on 6 August 1992. The Y&NM board room was on the first floor of the centre block. This room is now occupied by Route Control. Note, also, the 1906 NER headquarters building in the background. *Mrs C. A. Appleby*

Below:
The second Andrews' 'archway' of 1845, seen looking through Queen Street bridge towards the south end of the 1877 station and its car park on 6 August 1992. The platform and canopy to the left belonged to the now disused signals stores. *Mrs C. A. Appleby*

jointly operated (and financed) in conjunction with the Great North of England Railway (GNE) which was then in the process of building a line from Croft (a short distance south of Darlington) towards York.

The architect responsible for designing the station (and the archways through the city walls) was George Townsend Andrews (1804-1855), who subsequently carried out a lot of design work for railways within the Hudson sphere of influence, though his first attempt was vetoed by the ever cautious Darlington-orientated GNE Board of Directors, some of whom were also Directors of the Stockton & Darlington Railway and tended to look askance at Hudson's obvious liking for ostentation. Indeed, it was only after the submission of revised designs by Andrews that final agreement was reached between the Y&NM and GNE companies in March 1840, thus allowing tenders for construction to be invited. The station opened for Y&NM trains on 4 January 1841, and GNE passenger services from Darlington commenced on 30 March 1841.

The main building is a large two-storey structure, and faces towards Tanner Row; it contained both passenger facilities and offices with the booking hall situated in the centre. The upper

floor housed the Board Room (occupied by Regional Control – or Route Control as it is now called), and the half-yearly meeting of the Y&NM Board held on 29 January 1841 – presided over by George Hudson – was the first to take place there. The train shed behind the offices had a platform along each interior wall: the departure platform was situated immediately adjacent to the booking hall and offices, the arrival platform being on the opposite side. Whilst the facilities and amenities so far provided were doubtless sufficient for the level of activity prevailing in 1841, they soon were to become inadequate as the railway network around York grew from the mid-1840s onwards. Moreover, it was apparent that provision needed to be made for dealing with goods traffic, so on 22 April 1841 a tender was accepted for the construction of a 'merchandise station' and this building remained in use, latterly known as the 'Sack Warehouse' until it was demolished during the mid-1960s. The Y&NM also established coal and lime depots within the city walls on sidings which ran towards the river, and a large house was built for senior personnel which nowadays is called Toft Green Chambers and serves as BR office accommodation. Meanwhile, the GNE constructed a short line from North

Junction (now York Yard South) which gained access to their coal depots, together with a staith on the river bank where Durham coal could be tipped into vessels on the Ouse. These depots were located on land between the present Lendal Bridge (road) and Scarborough Bridge (rail), and they remained in use until the early 1870s when the access tracks were severed during site clearance in readiness for building the new station and hotel.

By the time the York-Scarborough line was opened on 7 July 1845, the need for additional facilities arose yet again. One major problem was the restricted rail access, governed by the archway through the city walls, which greatly inhibited the efficiency of operations, so this was resolved by breaching the city walls once more. The second (southernmost) archway, of identical design to the first, was constructed during 1845 and brought into use along with other associated track layout alterations in 1846. These improvements also included the provision of a double line curve between North Junction (York Yard South) and Holgate

Below:
A vintage photograph of the Y&NM carriage sidings taken from the city walls in 1868, looking towards Lendal Bridge and York Minster. Originally these were the Y&NM's coal depot sidings. *Crown Copyright; NRM, York*

Junction, thus creating a through north-south route. Two new platforms – known as the 'Scarborough Bays' – were added around this time to deal with the additional traffic generated by the opening of the Scarborough branch, and before long the station had to accommodate more services as the lines to Market Weighton (1847) and Knaresborough (1848) were opened, culminating in trains to and from the Doncaster direction (1850).

The two new platforms were formed outside the 1841 train shed, between the original arrival platform and the city walls, which involved cutting back the earth ramparts of the walls in order to build a retaining wall high enough to support one side of the new roof.

Certain buildings were also extended during this period; for instance, the Refreshment Room block on the arrival side had an upper floor added to cater for the influx of customers during 'refreshment stops' made by long distance trains. It must be remembered that this was the pre-dining car era so the lengthy stops for refreshments made at places such as York (and Preston to quote another example), usually resulted in an unholy scramble while a train-load of passengers endeavoured to satisfy their hunger and thirst within, say, an interval of 20min. Contemporary accounts tell us that Queen Victoria patronised these premises and enjoyed a (rather more leisurely?) meal there during her

train journey northwards on 28 September 1849 to open the High Level Bridge at Newcastle. On 22 February 1853 a station hotel was opened, built in a somewhat cramped position across the terminal ends of the platforms to a design by G. T. Andrews. (Perhaps this was the last major piece of railway design work to be carried out by Andrews, who received very few commissions from the Y&NM following Hudson's downfall in 1849, and who died in 1855 at the comparatively early age of 51.) The new hotel proved to be a big success, and following another visit by Queen Victoria during September 1854, it shortly afterwards assumed the name 'Royal Station Hotel'. This hotel building still exists, having been used as railway office accommodation since the new Royal Station Hotel (adjacent to the present station) opened in 1878, and it now forms part of the BR Headquarters complex being known as 'West Offices'.

As railways generally expanded from the 1850s onwards, and the volume of traffic increased, the difficulties associated with the operation of a terminus located on what in effect was a through trunk route became intolerable. As long ago as 1852, the Great Northern (GN) had complained about the inadequacy of the situation at York, which was further exacerbated by the opening of a direct line from Doncaster via Selby in 1871. Furthermore, various Board of Trade

Inspecting Officers had been making unfavourable comments in their reports about a variety of accidents which occurred, mainly due to the numerous propelled movements involving loaded passenger trains, which of necessity were being made – sometimes over quite considerable distances.

Thus constrained by limitations of space, which precluded any achievement of significant and lasting improvement, construction of a new station, situated outside the city walls, represented the only realistic solution to the almost impossible operating problems, and parliamentary powers were sought during 1865 for this purpose.

The 'new' (present day) station duly opened on 25 June 1877 and immediately thereafter the 'old' station ceased to be used for normal passenger business, though for many years (right up to the 1960s in fact) the station area and its adjacent sidings were used for the storage of coaching stock vehicles. An occasional static exhibition was held in the old station from time to time (such as the Festival of Britain display in 1951), and for a few years following its introduction in 1956, the York-Inverness Car Sleeper service (later called Motorail) used one of the platforms as an end-loading facility. Other uses were also found for some of the ancillary buildings; for instance, the original First Class Refreshment Room housed the small exhibits section of the LNER Railway Museum between 1928 and 1966 (see Chapter 10), and it remains in use to the present day as BR's Medical Centre.

Then during the 1950s, several changes took place which culminated in the train shed being bridged over in 1956, thus joining together the two main blocks of the old station to provide additional office accommodation. Finally, in

Top left:
A similar view taken on 6 August 1992. Note the NER war memorial, designed by Edwin Lutyens (who was also responsible for the Whitehall Cenotaph in London), which was unveiled on 14 June 1924. *Mrs C. A. Appleby*

Above:
Entrance to the 'old' station building where the NER war memorial now stands. The building to the left, once a refreshment room and subsequently occupied by the LNER Museum small exhibits section, is now BR's Medical Centre. *Crown Copyright; NRM, York*

Left:
A vintage postcard, probably dating from before World War 1, which shows the 1877 station portico, the 1878 Royal Station Hotel, shunting operations in progress in the 'old' station yard and a corner of the 1906 NER Headquarters. *Author's Collection*

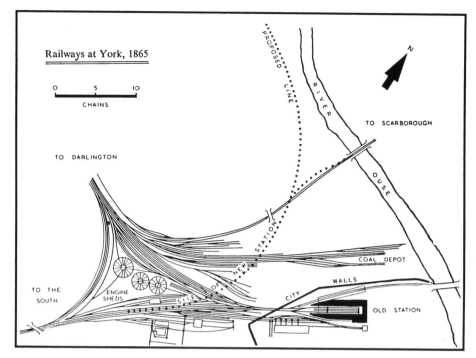

Railways at York, 1865

CHAINS

TO SCARBOROUGH

TO DARLINGTON

PROPOSED LINE

RIVER OUSE

SITE OF NEW STATION

COAL DEPOT

CITY WALLS

TO THE SOUTH

ENGINE SHEDS

OLD STATION

Left:
Railways at York in 1865.
Author's Collection

Below left:
Demolition of the 'old' station in progress during November 1966 in preparation for the building of Hudson House. The platform to the left was the 1845 extension to accommodate Scarborough branch trains. *BR*

Right:
A general view of the 'old' station area taken from the city walls on 6 August 1992. *Mrs C. A. Appleby*

celebrations which commemorated its establishment as 'Eboracum' in AD 71. Even Hudson Street, which became Railway Street after Hudson's fall from grace in 1849, was renamed George Hudson Street. The Adelphi Hotel at the corner of Micklegate assumed a new title – 'The Railway King' – and the Hudson residence at 44 Monkgate (now occupied by a firm of Accountants) received a commemorative plaque. Far from exonerating Hudson for the shady business practices which led to his removal from railway, civic and political life, at least a century after his death the part he played in putting York firmly on the railway map was finally recognised. Another famous railway personality of these times, who must not be overlooked, was George Leeman. Like Hudson, Leeman was three times Lord Mayor of York (though unlike Hudson, he was a Liberal) and he also became a Member of Parliament (for York). However, Leeman conducted his business affairs in a proper and respectable manner; he went on to become a Director of the NER in 1854 and rose to the position of Chairman (1874-1880).

Unlike his arch-rival Hudson, Leeman died rich and famous in 1882, and a statue of him which was erected in his honour now stands adjacent to the road bearing his name – which, incidentally, leads to the National Railway Museum.

The 'New' Station

During the latter part of 1866, after the NER's 1865 Parliamentary Bill had received the Royal Assent on 23 July, preliminary arrangements were made for the construction of a new station situated on land outside the city walls.

However, due to a trade recession which badly affected heavy industry throughout much of the northeast and thereby depressed the NER's freight revenue, coupled with a fall in share prices, (yes – these all too familiar sounding problems existed in those days as well!), it was considered prudent to defer work on a scheme of this magnitude until the financial position showed some sign of significant improvement. Eventually, work started in earnest during 1874 – an

the 1960s, the situation around the old station was irrevocably changed by removal of the tracks and a general site clearance which proceeded throughout much of 1966, in readiness for the construction of a large new office block to accommodate the technical departments of the soon to be merged Eastern and North Eastern Regions of BR (which took effect from 1 January 1967).

This huge complex, situated on the site of the former old station yard adjacent to G. T. Andrews' archways through the city walls, was built to a design approved by the Royal Fine Arts Commission and it contains four integrally linked office blocks, two of four storeys and two of six, with the tallest blocks being positioned

furthest away from the city walls so as to avoid them being dominated by the new buildings. Nevertheless, despite all the alterations that have been made over the years, one can still enjoy an overview of the old station and its surroundings by taking a leisurely stroll along the city walls between North Postern (next to Lendal Bridge) and Micklegate Bar. Also, a small portion of the original station roof still survives at the terminal end of the former train shed.

When opened on 7 November 1968 by Sir Henry Johnson, then BRB Chairman, the complex was named 'Hudson House' and it is of interest to note that, in 1971, Hudson's memory was 'rehabilitated' during the city's 1900th anniversary

Left:
Hudson's arch-rival George Leeman, Chairman of the NER 1874-1880, who died on 25 February 1882, is commemorated by this statue situated just outside the city walls. The statue is within sight of both the 'old' and 'new' stations as well as the 1906 Headquarters. It is also adjacent to Leeman Road, which leads to the National Railway Museum
Mrs C. A. Appleby

extension of powers had been obtained in 1871 as the five years allowed in the original Act had expired – and three years were to elapse before the present station was opened in all its glory on Sunday 25 June 1877, followed shortly afterwards by an equally impressive Royal Station Hotel (now the Royal York Hotel) on 20 May 1878.

The new station, with its magnificent curved roof, must have created quite an impression in its day. (It still does!). Indeed, as first built, the effect would have been strikingly symmetrical and pleasing to the eye, with its two lengthy through main platforms curved in an almost crescent shape, surmounted by a lofty overall roof of three elliptical spans. Deep bays, again of symmetrical appearance, adjoined the ends of both through platforms, and on the up (eastern) side there was a large circulating area which led to a spacious booking hall and portico. The walls were faced in a yellowish brick, and, despite numerous alterations carried out over the years, together with air-raid damage sustained on 29 April 1942, this massive edifice survives as a

lasting tribute to those who designed and built it.

Nevertheless, legend has it that a disaffected shareholder allegedly described the new station as 'a very splendid monument to extravagance', little thinking that before too many years were to elapse the volume of traffic would justify its enlargement.

The architect first responsible for the station's design was Thomas Prosser, who retired in 1874, though doubtless he was assisted by William Bell who subsequently became Chief Architect to the NER in 1877. Prosser was succeeded by Benjamin Burleigh, who died in 1876 and was followed by William Peachey to whom fell the task of seeing the work brought to a satisfactory conclusion. Whilst the finished job was more or less completed to Prosser's original design, Peachey was responsible for designing the adjacent Royal Station Hotel.

The impressive glazed roof over the train shed is 800ft long and 234ft wide; it consists of a 81ft span (48ft high) over the through platforms and tracks, with a 55ft span (40ft high) on each side. There is also a 43ft span (36ft high) on the east side, but this is bisected in the centre by the main block of station buildings. The wrought iron ribs of the roof are supported by massive cast iron columns, and the picturesque end screens, originally made of wood with glazed inserts, were renewed with aluminium framings as recently as 1972/73.

In its original form, the station had a total of 13 platforms – two long through platforms, five bays at the south end and six at the north. In addition, there were two through tracks (up and down main

Above:
An early photograph of the 1877 station looking north from the centre of No 4 platform (No 8 from 1938 and now No 3). The appearance of the coaches suggests that this is a 19th, rather than a 20th, century picture. Note the vintage semaphore signals and the lack of a footbridge. It is interesting to see the view of the station uncluttered with the footbridge; this was only provided when Platform 14 was constructed in 1900.
Author's Collection

Left:
Another early view of the 1877 station looking south along the then Platform 4.
Author's Collection

lines) in the centre. The bay platforms were originally numbered from east to west at the south end, thus Nos 1, 2 & 3 were east of the main up platform No 4, and Nos 6 & 7 were west of main down platform No 5. Conversely, the north end bays were numbered from west to east, so Nos 8 & 9 were west of No 5 platform and Nos 10, 11, 12 & 13 were east of No 4 platform. Nos 8 & 9 bays were only accessible to and from the north; Nos 10-13 bays, on the other hand, only gave access to and from the Scarborough direction.

As built in 1877, the platforms extended for only a short distance outside the main train shed. However, as trains became longer, the platforms at the south end were extended twice in the early years of this century. The last occasion in 1909 increased the main up platform length to 1,692ft. Furthermore, the low roof awnings which extend beyond the train shed (at both ends) also date from this period. Yet another feature of

the station's early days was that most Anglo-Scottish express trains still made extended stops at York for passengers to obtain food from the large dining and refreshment rooms then provided. Dining cars first appeared on certain East Coast route trains in 1893, but it was not until after 1900 that they gradually became universal on the principal main line services.

Below:
Old postcards invariably depicted interesting railway station scenes and this one taken of York is no exception. In particular, note that the station has now gained a footbridge. *Author's Collection*

Bottom:
The horse and cart era is very much in evidence. York station portico can be seen with the Royal Station Hotel in the background. *Author's Collection*

Left:
Looking south from York station c1907, with the second Locomotive Yard signalbox (1877-1909) to the right of the signal gantry. Note the position of the building to the right of the photograph; it was parallel to the original GNE line from the north to the old station, which ran across this site and had to be severed during the building of the 1877 station. *LPC/Ian Allan Library*

Below left:
A traditional view looking towards the south end of York station, again showing the second Locomotive Yard box. *LPC/Ian Allan Library*

Bottom:
Another old postcard looking from Holgate Bridge Junction towards the 1877 station and the South Sheds. Obviously 19th century judging by the look of the signals (with lamps positioned below the arms); also from the appearance of the freight train approaching from the direction of North Junction (York Yard South). *R. D. Pulleyn Collection*

On the initial 1871 plans, a proposed 'Excursion Platform' was shown to be situated immediately outside the western wall of the train shed. In the event, this facility was not provided until 1900 when, in anticipation of large crowds expected to attend the Royal Agricultural Show held at York that year, a temporary wooden platform was erected which then became No 14.

Subsequently, the new No 14 platform was used by the majority of northbound East Coast route trains, all of which involved a change of engines.

Pre-1900, the two sides of the station were connected by pedestrian subways, but concurrently with the provision of No 14 platform a footbridge was erected. From 1 September 1930, when the ticket barriers were repositioned to allow free access to the bookstall and refreshment rooms, the footbridge was moved a few yards northwards to its present position.

Another interesting addition to the station buildings was the 'Tea Room' which eventually became a railway staff canteen during, and for many years after, World War 2. Later, the 'Tea Room' was used as a relics shop, and even later still as a depot for the storage and issue of railway uniforms, but now it houses an imposing display of working model railways which is open to the public. Formerly 'Rail Riders World', this exhibition is now known as 'York Model Railway'.

Significant track layout alterations took place in association with the building of the new station. Towards the south end of the site, the 1841 GNE line between North Junction (York Yard South) and the old station was severed,

and at the north end the former Y&NM Scarborough line from North Junction crossed the new stretch of main line on the level at what soon became known as 'Waterworks Crossing'. Before reaching the bridge over the River Ouse, ('Scarborough Bridge' as it is known locally), the various connections to and from the new station joined the original route, and thereafter the North Junction-Waterworks portion of line became used for freight only. To carry the Scarborough branch across the River Ouse, a cast iron bridge had been built in 1845, but in 1874, in connection with the preparatory work for the new station, the bridge was rebuilt (in wrought iron) using the existing abutments and centre pier.

While major alterations to the track layout also took place at the south end of the station, leading up to the 1909 resignalling scheme – to be described in

York Station from Holgate.

rk. View from Holgate Railway Bridge.

Above:

This old postcard is especially interesting as it shows a corner of the very tall Holgate Bridge box, which was closed on 6 June 1909 when the third Locomotive Yard box was opened. (Note, also, the Great Northern train.)
R. D. Pulleyn Collection

Below:

A fascinating aerial photograph of York station, probably taken in the 1920s, if the types of motor vehicles lined up opposite are anything to go by.

Noteworthy locations are: 1. The two archways through the city walls; 2. Railway Institute; 3. Queen Street workshops buildings; 4. Site of later Platforms 15/16 (now Nos 10/11); 5. Branches Yard and Leeman Road coal depots; 6. Goods station office block (Now the National Railway Museum's Peter Allen building); 7. York North MPD (now the site of the National Railway Museum); 8. Waterworks crossing with Leeman Road box to the left and Waterworks (old) box to the right. *Aerofilms*

Chapter 6 – the next important event in the story of York station was the extensions on the west side undertaken between 1936 and 1939. On 9 July 1936, a formal ceremony took place to mark the commencement of the new extensions scheme, during which the first sod was cut by Thomas Hornsby – then Divisional General Manager of the LNER (NE Area).

A new island platform, some 1,180 ft in length, was to be constructed opposite to No 14 platform, complete with waiting rooms and a station buffet. Beyond that, a dock, (the 'Fruit Dock'), was to be constructed to deal with the transhipment of perishable traffic, which passed by rail in large quantities those days. Also included was a major resignalling scheme, (explained fully in Chapter 6), designed to replace all the manual signal boxes in the York Station area by colour light signals and electrically operated points controlled by one centrally located power signal box. The new island platform, numbered 15 & 16, became partially operative from 3 April 1938 when No 15 was temporarily connected through at the south end. No 16 came into use during March 1939, but effectively it was a bay platform accessible at the north end only. The outbreak of World War 2 in 1939 caused work on the York resignalling to be suspended. and No 16 did not become a through platform until final completion of the scheme in 1951. However, the proposed improvements

affecting Platform 14, (temporary since 1900!), were carried out during 1937/38, and an extension to the footbridge to give access to the new island platform was provided around the same time.

During the course of these prewar alterations, it was decided to simplify matters by renumbering the platforms, thus the low numbers 1-8 were all on the east side of the station, and the high numbers 9-16 on the west side, which took effect from 26 September 1938. But, to take this particular part of the story forward to the present day, the platforms were again renumbered from 14 May 1989 (in connection with the recent pre-electrification and resignalling work described in Chapter 7), which produced four instances where certain platforms actually reverted to their original 1877 numbering. Conversely, certain platforms were taken out of use – as the following comparative details show – and henceforward, to avoid confusion, platforms will be referred to in the narrative by their present-day numbers, along with the pre-1989 numbering in brackets immediately afterwards:

Renumbering of York Station Platforms

Present (14.05.89)	Former (26.09.38)	Original (25.06.1877)
-	1(+)	1
-	2	2
1	3	3
2	7	10
3	8	4
4	8B-(*)	4-(North)
5	9	5
6	10	6
7	11	7
8	13	8
-	12	9
9	14	(new in 1900)
10	15	(new in 1938)
11	16	(new in 1938)
-	6	11
-	5	12
-	4	13

Notes:

(+) Dispensed with in 1966. Used as Motorail-loading dock thereafter.

(*) Former 8 South and 8 North became 8A and 8B respectively from 5 May 1975.

Left:
A mid-1950s aerial photograph which gives a panoramic view of the general railway layout. Of particular note are: 1. South end of 1877 station; 2. Queen Street; 3. Erecting shops at former Loco Works; 4. Y&NM former Loco Works; 5. Holgate Villa offices; 6. Holgate Junction; 7. South Sheds; 8. Public footbridge; 9. Carriage Works; 10. Wagon Works; 11. Footbridge joining the Carriage Works and Wagon Works (since demolished); 12. Down Yard; 13. Up Yard; 14. York Yard North; 15. Skelton; 16. River Ouse; 17. Clifton Carriage Sidings; 18. Civil Engineers Yard; 19. Coaling plant at York North MPD; 20. Goods Warehouse, Leeman Road; 21 Branches Yard. *Author's Collection*

Right:
Later the same day (29 April 1942), the area had been tidied up and the sign indicated the way to alternative temporary facilities. Note the damaged roof support pillar shored up with a baulk of timber. *BR*

Below:
Disaster struck during the early hours of Wednesday 29 April 1942. The severity of the air-raid damage in the vicinity of the then Platforms 1-3 and around the Parcels Office area is vividly depicted in this official LNER photograph. *BR*

Right:
A present-day photograph of the damaged roof support column on 6 August 1992. This postwar replacement is the only one on the station which lacks the decorative capital of 'acanthus leaves'.
Mrs C. A. Appleby

Disaster overtook York station during an air-raid in the early hours of 29 April 1942. The overnight 10.15pm King's Cross-Edinburgh sleeping car train was standing in Platform 5 (9) when the bombs rained down on the station (and the motive power depot), and although a number of vehicles were removed (due to courageous actions performed by certain members of staff), six coaches were burned out right down to the frames and bogies.

Serious damage was caused to parts of the station roof, and at the inner end of No 1 (3) bay platform, one of the cast iron columns was totally destroyed by a high explosive bomb. Severe fire damage, caused by incendiaries, gutted many buildings, including the Booking and Parcels Offices; nevertheless, temporary

Above:

An exterior view taken later in the day on 29 April 1942. An alternative Parcels Office had by then been set up in Tea Room Square (towards the other end of the station). *BR*

Below:

By the next day, 30 April 1942, the debris had been cleared away. *BR*

Right:

An interesting photograph taken on 6 February 1948 looking south along the then Platforms 8 and 9. Note the NER Southern Division slotted post lower quadrant semaphores, complete with finials, which were worked by Platform box. These signals were cantilevered out from the ornate cast iron brackets that carried the original signals shown in earlier photographs. *BR*

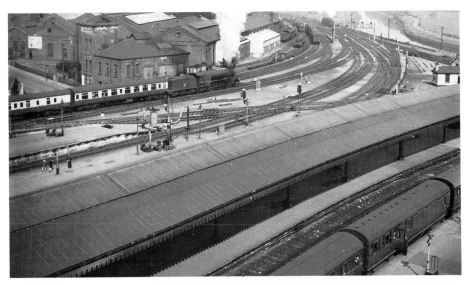

Right:
York station north end on 22 May 1956 taken from the Royal Station Hotel tower looking towards York (North) MPD and the present day NRM site.
J. W. C. Halliday

remedial measures were soon undertaken to maintain services, though several years were to elapse before permanent repairs were carried out. The location of the destroyed roof column referred to earlier can still be identified adjacent to the buffer stops of Platform 1 (3), because its postwar replacement lacks the decorative embellishment as cast at the top of the original. (The cast iron columns are crowned by elaborate capi-

Above:
Making a start on provision of car parking facilities at York station on 18 May 1966. The tracks in the foreground leading to and from the old station were lifted shortly afterwards. *BR*

Above right:
Mr John Shannon, Chairman of the York Civic Trust, is seen on 2 June 1971 while having a close look (with obvious approval!) at the detailed painting carried out by BR on the NER badges cast into the spandrels of York station roof. The shields represent the three main constituents of the NER: *top –* **Y&NM;** *left –* **LN;** *and right –* **YN&B.** *BR*

Below:
The line-up for the York station Centenary Exhibition is pictured at the former Platform 6 on 11 June 1977. Note the 1895 'railway races' veteran NER Class M1 4-4-0 No 1621. *David Bailey*

tals of 'acanthus leaves'; as originally constructed these were cast in sections and bolted into position.)

Station lighting was initially by gas supplied from the NER's own gas works located near to Severus Junction (now York Yard North), being replaced by electricity in 1957. Then, in 1975, the present sodium lighting was installed which provides a very high standard of illumination. Another important feature of the station's amenities is the announcing system, first introduced at York in 1927. Over the years, the system has gradually been updated and improved, and, to further enhance the quality of information for customers, television screens were first introduced in 1975. Here again, the system has recently been replaced by two large electronic information displays; one on the concourse facing the

entrance to Platform 3 (8), and the other within the circulating area on Platform 5 (9). These are supplemented by numerous smaller displays on screens located at various points throughout the station.

Finally, it is of interest to note that adjacent to the footbridge one can observe what appear to be coats of arms painted in colour on the roof spandrels. These heraldic devices depict the coats of arms adopted by the three main constituents which formed the NER (ie: Y&NM, Y&NB and LN), but in reality, none of these old constituent companies had permission from the College of Heralds to use such designs – nor did the NER seek to legalise the combined version used after 1854. The heraldic devices, therefore, are not 'crests' or 'coats of arms' but merely badges – in effect, little more than trade marks.

3. Passenger Services - An Overview 1839 to the 1960s

In 1839, the first passenger trains to be operated by the Y&NM Railway ran between York and Milford Old Junction (now called Gascoigne Wood), where connections for either Leeds or Selby could be made with services provided by the Leeds & Selby Railway, which had opened five years previously in 1834. Then, in 1840, after the Y&NM had completed its main line towards Normanton, a York-Leeds service was introduced which used a rather circuitous route via Whitwood Junction (Castleford) and Methley Junction to join the North Midland line into Leeds (Hunslet Lane) – and subsequently to Wellington station, situated in the centre of Leeds.

Rail travel between York and London (Euston Square) first became possible from 1 July 1840, by changing trains at Normanton and Derby. Initially, four services were provided, one of them involving an overnight journey, and the overall timings varied between 10 and 12hr – painfully slow by present day standards but a terrific improvement upon the stage coach.

Then, as the new mode of transport developed, and the Great Northern Railway had established itself at King's Cross in 1852, through services were provided. York-London journey times were progressively reduced, so that by 1870, (the final year that the GN main line services ran via the Askern-Knottingley route), the best timings had come down to 4hr 40min, which in those days must have seemed amazing. Indeed, after the Doncaster-York direct route via Selby opened in 1871, the fastest schedules were further reduced to 4¼hr – twice as long as the majority of InterCity services nowadays, but still quite impressive at the time, considering that railways in general had only been around for less than 50 years.

Going northwards, the GNE initially operated five services between York and Darlington, of which all except one called at the numerous intermediate stations *en route* and took about 2½hr for the 44-mile journey – very poor compared with InterCity's best timings of 27-29min, but a great advance upon the horse-drawn alternatives then available. In June 1844, as the railway system progressively expanded north of Darlington, the service from York was extended to Gateshead, and by 1848 to Edinburgh and Glasgow, with the opening of temporary bridges across the Rivers Tyne and Tweed (pending completion of permanent structures shortly afterwards).

By the mid-1850s, Anglo-Scottish passenger traffic along the East Coast route had developed into quite a substantial business, so much so that the three main companies involved (ie, GN, NER and the North British) reached an agreement (signed in November 1855) whereby they would work together for their mutual benefit. Five years later, a further agreement established a common stock of vehicles reserved exclusively for East Coast through traffic – thus was born the 'East Coast Joint Stock' (ECJS) concept. Initially, a pool of 50 new coaches and brake vans was put into traffic during 1861 (all four wheelers in those days), and the cost of joint use was divided between the three companies in proportion to their route mileage. Bogie vehicles were built from 1893 onwards. Right up to the end of 1922, 'ECJS' coaches were a familiar sight on the ECML, but after the 1923 Grouping the three parties to the agreement became part of the newly formed LNER.

The original branch line services of the 1840s radiated from York to Scarborough, Market Weighton and Knaresborough. Scarborough soon became a fashionable seaside resort, popular both for long-stay holidays and day trips, thus a greatly increased level of service came to be provided – especially during the summer months. Connections were made at Malton for Pickering and Whitby, together with some through services to Whitby eventually being provided during the peak summer season. The Market Weighton branch services were extended to Hull in 1865 with the opening of the Market Weighton-Beverley section, and a direct York-Hull service, which gave connections to and from the north, lasted until 1965. The Knaresborough branch service was extended to Harrogate in 1862.

Then in 1869, a dramatic improvement to the York-Leeds service became possible by the opening of Leeds 'New' Station (immediately adjacent to the Midland Railway's Wellington station), which was jointly owned by the London & North Western and North Eastern companies. At the same time, a new line was opened between Church Fenton and Micklefield, and the original Leeds & Selby Railway – which had an inconveniently located terminus at Marsh Lane – was extended into Leeds. Finally, the last addition to the branch line network from York came in 1875 with the introduction of through trains to Pickering via Helmsley.

Another major event which influenced the development of York's passenger train services, was the opening of the Swinton & Knottingley Joint Line in 1879. Jointly owned by the Midland and North Eastern, the S&K ran from Wath Road Junction (located north of Swinton on the former North Midland main line from Derby to Leeds), to Ferrybridge where a junction was made with the ex-Y&NM branch between Burton Salmon and Knottingley. The Midland soon built up a network of services, many running through to and from Bristol, Birmingham and London (St Pancras). Twenty years later, in 1899, the Great Central developed a variety of long distance express services using its then newly opened 'London Extension' as a means of gaining access to diverse places such as Bournemouth and Barry Island via a connection with the Great Western at Banbury. The GC came on to the S&K Joint Line at Dearne Junction (near Mexborough).

Naturally, the NER derived great benefit from these additional services

worked by other companies trains, as they brought in extra business. Indeed, in many ways, the legendary aspirations ascribed to George Hudson (of making all the railways come to York!) came somewhat nearer to fruition, in that by the end of the 19th century a total of six separate companies worked their own trains into York by virtue of Running Powers Agreements. A wide variety of different coloured locomotives and coaches were to be seen at York in those days; in fact, York was second only to Carlisle which played host to no less than seven pre-Grouping companies.

To summarise, in chronological order, the running powers exercised by these various companies – the Great Northern came first:

1. Great Northern Railway (GN)

On 25 November 1848, the Y&NM reached an agreement with the GN regarding through traffic between York and Doncaster; four GN engines would be stationed at York and two Y&NM engines at Doncaster. This was ratified by a supplementary agreement dated 25 November 1850, and allowed the GN to exercise running powers over the Y&NM – and subsequently the NER – between Knottingley and York. A revised agreement on 15 March 1864 made provision for the GN to run over the NER between Shaftholme Junction and York via Selby, and these powers were duly exercised (for both passenger and freight traffic) from the opening of the new route on 2 January 1871.

2. Midland Railway (MR)

By an agreement made on 30 October 1874, the Midland obtained running powers over the NER from Altofts Junction (Normanton) and Methley Junction to York, but these were not exercised. The same agreement also made provision for the Midland to enjoy running powers (for both passengers and freight) over the NER between Ferrybridge and York, and these rights were duly exercised after the S&K Joint line was opened to freight on 19 May 1879, and for passengers on 1 July 1879.

3. Lancashire & Yorkshire Railway (L&Y)

The L&Y commenced working passenger trains between Normanton and York on 1 May 1884, and the arrangement was duly ratified by an agreement made on 5 February 1886. (The agreement was extended to include cattle traffic in 1896.)

4. Great Eastern Railway (GE)

An agreement made on 24 March 1893 confirmed the fact that the GER had commenced working certain passenger trains between Doncaster and York from 1 November 1892. (These trains were worked to and from GE territory proper at March over the GN/GE Joint line via Lincoln.)

5. London & North Western Railway (LNW)

From 1 July 1893, the LNW extended three of their Liverpool-Leeds services and worked them to York, following an agreement reached on 17 June 1893. However, this arrangement was short-lived, and the LNW ceased to exercise their running powers to York on 31 December 1904.

6. Great Central Railway (GC)

As the final 'foreign' company to come to York, the GC reached agreement with the NER on 1 December 1898 for running powers (passenger traffic) between Ferrybridge and York (to Milford only for freight), which were exercised from 15 March 1899. (GC trains ran over the S&K Joint Line between Dearne Junction and Ferrybridge.)

After the Grouping took place in 1923, the London Midland & Scottish Railway (LMS) continued to exercise the running powers it had inherited from the Midland and L&Y companies. The other companies mentioned, (ie, GN, GE and GC), became part of the London & North Eastern Railway (LNER).

From 1932 onwards the LNER accelerated some of the more prestigious main line services, such as the time-honoured 'Flying Scotsman', but without doubt the highlights of the 1930s were the streamlined trains of the H. N. (later Sir Nigel) Gresley high-speed era. The first of these famous prewar trains, which entered public service on Monday 30 September 1935, was the 'Silver Jubilee' – so named to commemorate the Silver Jubilee of King George V – and its luxurious new set of coaches finished in a very striking silver-grey livery. The 'Silver Jubilee' was hauled by equally distinctive streamlined Class A4 locomotives, of which four were specially built bearing the names: *Silver Link* (No 2509), *Quicksilver* (No 2510), *Silver King* (No 2511) and *Silver Fox* (No 2512).

Running in previously unheard of schedules, giving an overall average speed of 67.08 mph in each direction, the up (southbound) 'Jubilee' left Newcastle at 10.0am, and after only one stop at Darlington (10.40-10.42), was due to arrive at King's Cross at 2.0 pm. In the down (northbound) direction, the 'Jubilee' left King's Cross at 5.30 pm and after one stop at Darlington (8.48-8.50pm), was due to arrive at Newcastle at 9.30pm. Neither train was booked to call at York, and they passed through at 11.19am (up), and 8.9pm (down) respectively, which called for a high degree of co-ordination between the then manually operated signal boxes in and around the station area in order to ensure a clear road.

Hard on the heels of the 'Jubilee' came another equally famous streamlined service, the 'Coronation', introduced from 5 July 1937, so named to mark the Coronation of King George VI. Two new trains of luxury coaches finished in light and dark blue (or 'garter' blue) livery were needed for the two 'Coronation' trains; meanwhile, the construction of

Above:
The prewar 'Silver Jubilee' was a marvellous sight. Here No 2512 *Silver Fox* accelerates away after passing through York station on the Up Main, probably in 1936 or 1937. The photograph was certainly taken prior to the 1938 signalling alterations at Locomotive Yard box. *H. Gordon Tidey*

further Class A4 locomotives had been undertaken. Five of the new 'A4s' were specially named after Empire, Dominion or Commonwealth countries: *Union of South Africa* (No 4488), *Dominion of Canada* (No 4489), *Empire of India* (No 4490), *Commonwealth of Australia* (No 4491) and *Dominion of New Zealand* (No 4492). The down (northbound) train left King's Cross at 4.0pm, and it was booked to call at York (6.37-6.40pm), then non-stop to Edinburgh, arriving at 10.0pm. Subsequently, from 7 March 1938, a Newcastle stop was also included. In the up (southbound) direction, the 'Coronation' did not call at York and passed through at 7.53pm.

Regrettably, the excitement of the Gresley high-speed era was all too soon brought to an abrupt end by the outbreak of World War 2 in 1939. Inevitably the prestige streamlined services were suspended 'for the duration' – and, in the event, were never to be resumed.

Nevertheless, during their relatively brief period of operation, these particular trains demonstrated the progress made by our railways at that time; in the context of speed and comfort they were superb (InterCity nowadays provides this standard of service as matter of course).

After World War 2, main line services took some time to recover anything

approaching prewar standards of speed and service, bearing in mind the arrears of maintenance to be made up following an almost six year period of abnormally high wartime traffic levels. Nonetheless, it is of interest to note that something of the prewar streamlined atmosphere was recreated when in 1953, the non-stop 'Elizabethan' was introduced with an overall timing of 6³/4 hr in each direction. Actually, the 'Elizabethan' was an accelerated version of the former 'Capitals Limited' renamed in honour of the present Queen's Coronation.

Branch lines around York settled down into a generally uneventful existence from the 1923 Grouping onwards, though for a few years during the 1920s experiments were conducted with short distance local trains; these were often worked by push and pull units (or 'Autocars' in North Eastern terminology), or occasionally by petrol driven or 'Sentinel' (steam) railcars. For example, the summer timetable of 1927 showed a local service on the York end of the Scarborough branch operating between York and Flaxton.

Also, 1927 saw the start of the Rowntrees' passenger services which ran between York and a newly constructed halt situated at Rowntrees' chocolate factory on Haxby Road, connected with the Foss Islands freight branch near to its junction with the Scarborough line at Burton Lane box. (This service, once very well patronised but latterly not so, survived until the last train ran on Friday afternoon 8 July 1988.) The local services to Haxby, Strensall and Flaxton eventually succumbed to competition from rapidly developing bus operators and from 22 September 1930, all the intermediate stations on the York-Scarborough branch – except Malton and Seamer – were closed to passengers.

Other notable changes to branch line services affecting York were the withdrawal of the York-Pickering via Helmsley trains, which ran for the last time on Saturday 31 January 1953, the Malton-Whitby trains on Saturday 6 March 1965, and the direct service to Hull via Pocklington and Market Weighton, which ceased after the last trains ran on Saturday 27 November 1965.

YORK AND FLAXTON

		WEEKDAYS																			SUNDAYS	
			X	X	A SO X	SX X		X	SO	X		X		SO X	SX X		SO	SO			
		a.m	a.m	a.m	a.m	p.m	p.m	p.m	p.m	p.m	p.m	p.m	p.m	p.m	p.m	p.m	p.m	p.m	p.m	a.m	a.m
YORK ....dep		6 45	8 8	1025	1113	1255	*1 15*	2 7	3 10	3 50	4 23	5 13	6 23	7 5	8 50	9 40	9 40	1030		8 30	10 15
Haxby .... „		6 54	8 17	1035	1123	1 4	*1 25*	2 17	3 20	3 59	4 33	5 22	6 33	7 14	9 0	9 50	9 50	1039		8 39	.....
Strensall Halt .... „		....	8 23	1041	1129	....	*1 31*	2 23	3 26	....	4 39	....	6 39	....	9 6	9 56	....	....		.....	.....
Strensall .... „		6 59	8 25	1043	1131	1 9	*1 33*	2 25	3 28	4	4 41	5 *t*38	6 41	7 19	9 8	9 58	9 57	1044		8 44	10 26
FLAXTON .... arr.		7 5	—	—	1138	1 15	—	—	3 35	*4 10*	4 48	5 44	—	7 25	—	—	—	—		8 50	—

		WEEKDAYS																	SUNDAYS	
			X	X	B SO	A SO X	SX X		X	X		X		SO X	SO	SX X			
		a.m	a.m	a.m	a.m	p.m	p.m	p.m	p.m	p.m	p.m	p.m	p.m	p.m	p.m	p.m	p.m	p.m	p.m
FLAXTON ....dep		7 50	—	9 53	—	11 44	.....	.....	—	2 52	3 54	4 54	5 21	—	8 27	—	—	—	8 14
Strensall .... „		7 55	8 35	9 59	10 50	11 51	*1 11*	*1 37*	2 35	2 58	4 1	5	5 27	6 45	8 33	9 *12*	10 6	*t*0 6	8 20
Strensall Halt...... „		...	8 37	...	10 52	11 53	.....	*1 39*	2 37	...	4 3	5 3	...	6 47	...	9 14	...	*t*0 5	—
Haxby .... „		8 0	8 42	10 4	10 58	11 59	*1 16*	*1 45*	2 43	3 4	4 9	5 9	5 32	6 53	8 38	9 20	1012	*t*0 14	8 26
YORK .. .. arr.		8 12	8 51	10 13	11 8	12 10	*1 30*	*1 55*	2 53	3 12	4 19	5 19	5 41	7 3	8 47	9 31	1023	*t*0 24	8 35

A Runs on 16th July only.   **B** Commences 23rd July.   **SO** Saturdays only.   **SX** Saturdays excepted.
t Arrives 5.27 p.m.   **X** Rail Motor Bus. One class only.

Towards the end of the 1950s, steam began to lose its pre-eminence and diesel locomotives were gradually introduced into main line services from the 1958/59 timetable onwards. Diesel Multiple Units (DMUs) also appeared on local services around York towards the end of the decade, having first arrived on the Bradford Exchange-Leeds Central-Harrogate route in June 1954. Thus the scene was set for the transition from steam to diesel – a momentous period in railway history – which will be described more fully in Chapter 8.

Right:
'A4' No 4492 *Dominion of New Zealand* in garter blue livery hauling an ordinary express service past Holgate Excursion Platforms on 22 August 1937. *Ian Allan Library*

Above:
The 'A4s' built in 1937 for the 'Coronation' services were of truly impressive appearance. In this excellent shot of No 4492 *Dominion of New Zealand*, the Up 'Flying Scotsman' is seen approaching Clifton in 1938. *Crown Copyright; NRM, York*

Right:
Between 27 September 1937 and the outbreak of World War 2 in 1939, the Up 'Yorkshire Pullman' from Harrogate was routed via York and worked by Starbeck engines and crews to Doncaster. In this photograph, taken south of St Helens Road bridge, 'D20' No 1217 is piloting rebuilt 'D20' No 2020. *C. Ord*

Left:
Another classic photographic location was the space between the main line and No 2 Group sidings outside York (North) MPD. Class A3 No 2582 *Sir Hugo* heads a northbound express past Clifton box during the mid-1930s. *C. Ord*

Above:
Postwar express passenger services: Peppercorn 'A1' Pacific No 60120 *Kittiwake* heads the Up 'Northumbrian' past Holgate Excursion Platforms during the early 1950s. *C. Ord*

Left:
***Mallard*, renumbered from 4468 to 22 in the LNER revised system of numbering, passes the south end of York station on 25 September 1948 with the Down 'Flying Scotsman'.** *J. W. Armstrong*

Above:
Class A3 No 60072 *Sunstar* **heads the Up 'Tees-Tyne' Pullman service at Holgate Excursion Platforms during the early 1950s.** *C. Ord*

Left:
Another 'Northumbrian' photograph – this time the train is being hauled by 'A4' No 60003 *Andrew K. McCosh. C. Ord*

Below:
In 1953 the non-stop 'Elizabethan' was introduced to mark the occasion of our present Queen's Coronation. Another classic location shot of the down train passing Clifton hauled by No 60004 *William Whitelaw. C. Ord*

Inset left:
The up 'Elizabethan' passing the south end of York station hauled by 'A4' No 60012 *Commonwealth of Australia* **on 25 June 1956.** *L. Overend*

Left:
The final train departing from Rowntree's Halt on the afternoon of Friday 8 July 1988. Normally a two-car DMU was used for this service, but on this very last occasion demand from railway enthusiasts was such that a three-car set was provided! The Foss Islands branch remained open for occasional oil trains to serve the depot situated at the Layerthorpe end of the Derwent Valley Railway, but after the contract expired in October 1988 the branch fell into disuse. *D. S. Lindsey*

Above:
A Scarborough bound excursion leaving Platform 15 (now No 10) on 23 August 1960 hauled by Class B16/3 4-6-0 No 61472. Note some of the South Sheds buildings in the right background, also the wagons in the then South View sidings. *R. Leslie*

Above:
'B1' 4-6-0 No 61255 stands in the then Platform 6 at York station with a Hull train on 27 June 1964. The Royal Station Hotel is visible in the background. *N. F. W. Dyckoff*

Above:
Summer Saturday afternoon activity in 'Scarborough Corner' at York station on 13 July 1963. 'B1' No 61360 is ready to leave former Platform 4 with the 15.35 York-Whitby service. This train incorporated through coaches from King's Cross. Alongside, 'B16/2' No 61438 awaits to depart with the 15.40 service to Hull at the then Platform 6. At the time of writing, in September 1992, the former Platforms 4 and 5 are being filled in to provide much-needed additional 'short wait' car parking facilities.
J. M. Rayner

Left:
BR/Sulzer Type 4 No D38 waits to leave on 1 September 1962 from the south end of Platform 5 (9) with the 2.40pm Scarborough-Bristol service while 'A4' No 60013 *Dominion of New Zealand* pauses with a Glasgow Queen Street-King's Cross train on Platform 3 (8).
J. S. Whiteley

Right:
Another Treacy classic; this time taken at the south end of York station with an up express departing for King's Cross with 'A4' No 60018 *Sparrow Hawk* in charge during the mid-1950s. Note the South Sheds in the background.
Eric Treacy

Right:
While steam 'officially' disappeared from the East Coast main line in 1965, locomotives from London Midland Region depots could still be seen occasionally at York right up until the end of steam in 1968. Here the 17.45 (FO) from Manchester Exchange has just arrived at Platform 3 (8) on 9 July 1967 headed by Stanier 'Black 5' No 44727. *R. Tallet*

Below:
The late Eric Treacy regularly photographed trains at York, but unfortunately most of his superb photographs are undated. In this classic example of Treacy's photographic prowess, the up 'Flying Scotsman' hauled by 'A4' No 60017 *Silver Fox* is seen passing Clifton Carriage Sidings during the early 1950s. *Eric Treacy*

Above:
Treacy's speciality was to capture live steam in action, rather than photograph still shots. In this example, Class D49/2 4-4-0 No 62774 *The Staintondale* makes a spirited departure from York with a train for Harrogate in the early 1950s.
Eric Treacy

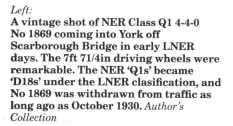

Left:
A vintage shot of NER Class Q1 4-4-0 No 1869 coming into York off Scarborough Bridge in early LNER days. The 7ft 7 1/4in driving wheels were remarkable. The NER 'Q1s' became 'D18s' under the LNER clasification, and No 1869 was withdrawn from traffic as long ago as October 1930. *Author's Collection*

Left:
A fine Treacy shot of 'A4' No 60022 *Mallard* passing the south end of Dringhouses Yard with the up 'Tees-Tyne' Pullman during the mid-1950s.
Eric Treacy

4. Freight Depots and Marshalling Yards

York cannot lay claim to being an industrial city, and much of its immediate hinterland is predominantly agricultural, yet in the days when the railways' only competitors were the horse and cart or water transport, a substantial amount of freight traffic passed by rail.

Originally, both the Y&NM and GNE companies established depots in York to deal with coal and lime, and before long, once the early railway system began to take shape, York was to become involved in dealing with a variety of long distance freight train services – a feature which has continued right up to the present day. Conversely, the extensive network of local freight trains and 'pickups' which once served the numerous branch lines and country stations in the vicinity have vanished from the scene for ever.

The largest flow of freight traffic originating at York was confectionery from Messrs Rowntrees, who, by 1891, had relocated to a large factory at what then was an 'out of town' site at Haxby Road, complete with an internal railway system, and a private siding connected with the NER's Foss Islands branch.

Another major event on the freight scene was the opening of the sugar beet factory in 1926. This too was a private siding, though, in this case, the traffic was largely seasonal in character, because the 'beet campaign' (as this seasonal activity was called) only lasted for a few months during the winter. Yet another significant freight activity which survived until comparatively recent years was cattle traffic – much of which came to York by ship and rail from Ireland and was dealt with at Foss Islands. In 1923, for example, York received 7,884 wagons of livestock, which made it second only to Newcastle in the LNER NE Area.

Much of York's inwards and outwards general merchandise was handled at a large goods depot at Leeman Road which dates from the 1890s, (a precise date has so far eluded the author), with some bulk traffic being dealt with at Foss Islands.

Above:
An early 20th century photograph of Leeman Road Goods Station office block and weighbridge. The main block is now the NRM's 'Peter Allen' building. The new entrance to the NRM is just off the picture to the right. *Crown Copyright; NRM, York*

However, following the 1968 Transport Act, one main effect of which was to separate the 'sundries' (or 'smalls') from 'full loads traffic' and to set up a 'Sundries Division' of BR – which subsequently became National Carriers Ltd (NCL) – BR handed over the Leeman Road goods station building and associated warehouse premises to NCL, and in 1972 concentrated its residual 'full loads' activities at Foss Islands. Nevertheless, within the space of a few years, NCL vacated much of the Leeman Road depot, thus during 1976 the premises were acquired by the National Railway Museum (NRM) – as described in Chapter 10 – and the main building was formally named (after himself) by Sir Peter Allen on 24 October 1979.

Since the 'Beeching' era of the mid-1960s, many radical changes affecting the freight scene at York have taken place, particularly so within most recent years, until the stage has been reached where nowadays there is virtually no commercial freight traffic either originating or received at York. On the other hand, many long distance train loads of bulk commodities like coal, oil, petroleum and metals pass through York, or are staged for crewing purposes. York no longer possesses either a freight depot or a marshalling yard as such, and virtually all the erstwhile private sidings have disappeared, yet there is still quite a lot of freight train activity to be seen – particularly around the York Yard North locality where most of the remanning and/or staging takes place.

Development of Freight Train Services

By the time that the NER established itself in 1854, it had become evident that the transport of freight by rail possessed enormous potential. Not only did the

Below:
Activity in the up arrivals at York Yard North on 17 September 1977. Class 37 No 37113 is seen coming off a staged freight, and Nos 37020/37283 are on a train of ore empties. *G. W. Morrison*

Left:
Looking beyond York Yard North towards Skelton in a view also taken on 2 June 1980. Down departures are seen to the left of the picture, goods lines (now slow lines) in the centre, up arrivals to the right and the East Coast main line to the extreme right. Note, also, the MGR wagons staged for working forward. *BR*

early railways around York provide freight services on their local lines, but also the benefits to be gained from block train working of through loads along what is now the ECML were soon to be realised. For example, it is known that by 1861, a 'Meat Train' at 3.55am from Newcastle was due in York at 8.30am, having stopped only at Darlington and Thirsk, and an 'Aberdeen Express Goods' was booked to leave Newcastle at 9.30am arriving in York at 2.15pm. There was also a 'Fish Train' from Newcastle at 3.10pm arriving in York at 7.40pm with three stops *en route*.

Numerous mineral trains had also appeared on the scene, described variously as 'Coke for Normanton' or 'GN

Coal', and there was even an example of what one might now regard as a 'Company Train' described as 'Cootes' Train'. (Coote was a coal merchant at St Ives near Huntingdon, who had a contract to supply large tonnages of coal from Peterborough to various stations on the then Eastern Counties Railway – later the Great Eastern.) Then, in 1872, ex-Stockton & Darlington (S&D) locomotives were known to be working through from Shildon to Hexthorpe (near Doncaster) on block train loads of Durham coke for the Manchester, Sheffield & Lincolnshire Railway (MS&L – later to become the Great Central), and by 1874 the traffic had grown to the extent that three daily services were justified.

By the end of the 19th century, really fast express freight services had appeared on the ECML and, according to the 1898 Appendix, such trains were designated 'SWB' (Special White Board) as the locomotive carried two white boards to indicate their status – one at the foot of the chimney and one at the centre of the front buffer beam. These trains were similarly designated in the Working Timetable (WTT), and even signalled on the block by a special bell code of five beats (given consecutively).

In LNER days, certain well known express freight services came into being. For instance, the famous prewar 3.40pm King's Cross-Niddrie 'flyer' (No 1 Braked Goods 421 Down) was scheduled to run from York Severus (now York Yard North) to Newcastle (Central) in 111min, and a 1934 main line WTT in the author's possession carries the exhortation 'Will take precedence over all trains except East Coast Passenger trains' as an indication of its priority. Similarly, in the up direction, the two equally prominent express meat and fish services from Aberdeen were given special treatment to emphasise their importance. 418 Up (10.45am Express MEAT) was allowed 101min from Newcastle to York and 490 Up (1.45pm Express FISH) was given 103min. Both trains were given the same degree of priority accorded to the Niddrie 'flyer' in the down direction.

The LNER was very keen to develop their premier freight services and an official publication issued in September 1938 entitled *How the LNER Expresses Freight,* detailed the various trains on offer to customers. The 3.40pm Niddrie had by then become the 3.35pm 'Scotsman', and the Northeast was served by two new trains from King's Cross Goods at 4.5pm and 5.15pm. In their heyday, these services (usually hauled by Gresley's then new mixed traffic 2-6-2 Class V2 locomotives) represented the ultimate in freight train operation. The majority of fast freights disappeared during World War 2, but they were gradually reintroduced from 1946 onwards.

Meanwhile, to revert to the ordinary and less spectacular freight train services for wagon load traffic, which increased significantly over the years commensurate with the general growth of rail traffic during the second half of the 19th century, York acquired a number of marshalling yards.

Marshalling Yards

The area between North Junction (York Yard South from October 1938) and Severus (known as York Yard North also from October 1938) is traditionally known as 'York Yards'. Various groups of sidings have been established in this particular locality from the early 1880s, and ever since the 1877 station was opened passenger trains have only traversed the York Yards area in the event of diversions for emergencies or engineering operations. Initially, York did not require the provision of extensive marshalling yards for through main line freight traffic, though many sidings were needed to stage or recess through loads while engines and/or crews were changed, for York was very much a 'frontier point' in this respect. (To some extent it still is.) Additionally, some marshalling and sorting activities began to take place from the 1870s onwards at peripheral yards like Thirsk and Milford, to quote just two examples. Towards the end of the 19th century, when ever increasing freight traffic flows from the industrial Northeast, particularly Tees-side, were encountered, even the construction of a large marshalling yard at Northallerton was seriously contemplated. (This yard, had it ever been built, would have been situated south of Northallerton on land between the ECML and the Leeds Northern lines.)

Nevertheless, York was the focal point of many branch lines and secondary routes in the vicinity, thus by the late 1880s both up and down yards had been constructed within the traditional 'York Yards' area, followed in the early 1890s by Branches Yard, together with Leeman Road coal depots, which were situated alongside the 'Scarborough' lines between North Junction (York Yard South) and the north end of the 1877 passenger station.

Further developments took place during and towards the end of World War 1 when greatly increased traffic volumes were encountered. Both Holgate Reception Lines and Dringhouses Yards date from this period. The four sidings at Holgate (now three), situated on the down side immediately south of Holgate Bridge, were originally intended as additional reception facilities for York No 1 Down Yard, though in practice they have always proved useful for staging purposes, or for temporary standage of coaching stock. The up and down yards at Dringhouses were constructed, it is to be believed, towards the end of World War 1.

Moving on to World War 2, even further increased traffic justified the construction of Skelton New Sidings, which opened towards the end of 1942. Not strictly speaking a marshalling yard as such, Skelton's principal function was the staging of through loads to be re-engined, thus six up and six down reception lines were provided together with two engine lines and associated facilities for watering and cleaning fires of locomotives.

To summarise, by 1948 when the railways were Nationalised, the undermentioned yards at York were operational:

York No 1	Down Yard (this was a hump yard);
York No 2	Down Yard ('Klondyke' – a flat yard);
York No 1	Up Yard (the remainder were all flat yards);
York No 2	Up Yard;
Warehouse	Yard (to serve Leeman Road goods depot);
Branches	Yard (as implied by its name to deal with pick ups etc);
Dringhouses	Down Yard (North traffic);
Dringhouses	Up Yard (South and West traffic).

Additionally, there were staging sidings at York Yard North, known as the Up Arrivals and Down Departures, also at Skelton and Holgate.

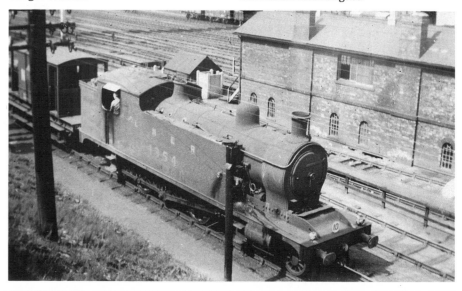

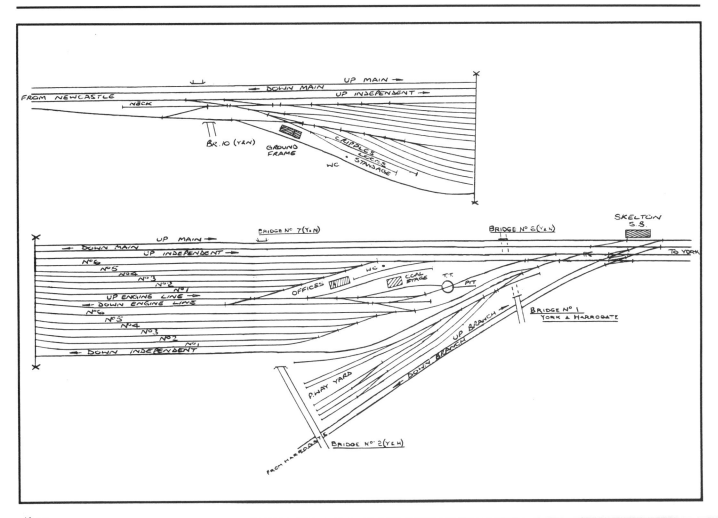

Above:
Skelton New Sidings. *Author's Collection*

Below left:
**NER Raven Class X (LNER Class T1)
4-8-0T No 1354 on hump shunting duties
in 1937 at York No 1 Down Yard. The
signal box in the background is the old
York Yard South. At the time this
photograph was taken this box was
called North Junction.** *Author's Collection*

Right:
**BR Standard Class 9F 2-10-0 No 92020 is
caught leaving Skelton New Sidings
with a southbound freight on 15 August
1964. The locomotive was originally
fitted with a 'Crosti' boiler, but
subsequently the 'Crosti' pre-heater was
sealed off for orthodox working.**
A. W. Martin

To service the various yards and sidings, no less than 18 shunting pilots were employed (many of which were treble shifted), with the addition of a 'Ferry' Pilot and three 'Running' pilots to deal with inter-yard trips, plus a dedicated Sugar Beet pilot during the beet season, and two pilots *each* for the Carriage Works and the Wagon Shops. Activity on this scale continued into the mid-1950s, then things began to alter as the whole of the then North Eastern Region freight operating strategy was redefined as a prelude to the forthcoming

modern yard era, accompanied by dieselisation, of the 1960s.

Clearly, a large modern marshalling yard could not be justified for York, though improvements to the Up Yard were carried out during 1958 when a 'mini' hump (or 'knuckle') was constructed and the sidings completely remodelled. However, the main event of the early 1960s was the reconstruction and enlargement of Dringhouses Up Yard, which then became the focal point for fitted freight trains from the industrial heartlands of the Northeast.

In fact, a contemporary press release issued by BR on 6 January 1962 claimed that Dringhouses Up Yard had the distinction of being the first yard in the country to deal exclusively with fully fitted express freights. During 1961, the yard was converted into a hump yard and at the same time the existing sidings were lengthened and nine additional roads provided.

An elevated control room was built at the north end of the yard, with the layout depicted on an illuminated panel, so that the operator could route the wagons into

Left:
The present-day scene at York Yard South on 6 August 1992 taken from the public footbridge next to the former Yard Master's office. Note the very much simplified layout. The land in the foreground is the site of the No 1 Down Yard Hump. *Mrs C. A. Appleby*

Centre left:
Looking the other way from the public footbridge in this pre-1962 York Yard South resignalling view, Class B16/1 4-6-0 No 61451 can be seen pulling out of South View sidings with a rake of wagons. Note, also, Branches Yard to the left of the picture (now a car park). The two running lines immediately to the left of the train were the 'Scarborough Goods Lines', and hereabouts was the site of the original North Junction when the Scarborough branch was first opened in 1845. *P. J. Lynch*

Below:
Another example of Treacy's excellent photographic work shows Stanier '8F' No 48119 leaving the south end of Dringhouses Yard during the early 1950s with a typical wagon-load freight train of that era. *Eric Treacy*

Below right:
Modernisation in progress at the north end of Dringhouses Up Yard during 1961. The steam cranes are laying in the new retarders. Note the hump control tower still under construction.
E. Sanderson

Above:
A late 1950s shot of 'Austerity' WD 2-8-0 No 90006 passing the south end of Dringhouses Yard on the up Leeds line with a train of mineral empties. Dringhouses Down Yard is to the left of the picture. *F. Ingham*

the appropriate sorting sidings and at the same time control their speed by means of hydraulically operated retarders. The yard was at its busiest during the late evening and throughout the night. By 1962, every weekday (except Saturdays), some 850 wagons arrived to be sorted into approximately 30 trains which were despatched during the night to the industrial centres of the Midlands, and a variety of destinations in the South and West Country.

Unfortunately, the 'expansionist boom' which followed in the wake of the 1955 Modernisation Plan was soon to be tempered by agonising reappraisals of policy which led ultimately to what has gone down in railway history as the 'Beeching' era of the 1960s. In any event, the traditional wagon load business – which had remained reasonably buoyant during much of the 1950s – began a downwards slide to oblivion. Furthermore, the effect of the so-called 'Beeching'-type cuts had resulted in the disappearance of much of the branch line freight traffic, thus it became painfully evident that rationalisation of York's extensive yards would soon follow.

During 1966, after track layout and signalling alterations were carried out, Dringhouses Up Yard became, in effect, an 'up and down' yard, which led to the closure of Dringhouses Down and York No 1 Down Yards. No 2 Down Yard was given over to the Civil Engineering Department; the Up Yard was henceforth used mainly for storage purposes, and Branches Yard, along with Warehouse Yard, was closed. By the end of the 1960s, only Dringhouses remained as a marshalling yard and was still very busy, especially between late afternoon and the early hours of the following morning. The staging sidings at Holgate, York Yard North and Skelton, together with an assortment of BR departmental sidings continued in use more or less as before.

Thereafter, further changes were mainly concerned with Freightliner and Speedlink services, and a lot of exchanging sections (as opposed to remarshalling) took place at Dringhouses during the 1970s. Also, as the train load concept developed, the instances of through engine workings increased, so gradually the numbers of trains requiring to be dealt with at York declined, unless a planned crew change was involved. Thus it was found possible to do without Skelton New Sidings, so prior to the major remodelling and resignalling at Skelton (which was commis-

sioned on 13 March 1977), they were closed during January 1977.

Another development of the mid-1970s arose from a further serious decline in the wagon load business. This led in 1977 to BR's decision to introduce a network of fast air-braked trunk freight services which became known as 'Speedlink'. In many ways, Speedlink closely resembled the pattern of fast freights which were the pride of the LNER from the 1930s. Like them, Speedlink services were usually long distance trains; rather than being re-formed at intermediate yards, they connected into/out of other such workings and exchanged sections with them, so hump shunting was not involved. Indeed, at that time, Dringhouses was one of the locations chosen to be a main network yard for Speedlink traffic. Yet within the space of a few more years, the death knell was tolled for the remaining wagon load traffic as the BRB Corporate Plan contained a declared objective that by May 1984 the intention was 'to phase out the non air-braked wagon load network completely'. Actually, humping at Dringhouses Yard (North End) ceased from 3 March 1985 thus the relatively modern hump tower fell into disuse, and in 1986 a proposal was developed to close Dringhouses altogether by 1989 (when York new signalling was due to be introduced) and transfer the remaining operations to the York Yard North area. However, subsequent events overtook this scheme, for towards the end of 1986 Railfreight's principal customer in York – Rowntree-Mackintosh (now called

Foss Islands Branch

Authorised under the NER New Lines Act of 16 July 1874, the Foss Islands branch diverged from the York-Scarborough line at Burton Lane Junction and ran to a freight depot in Foss Islands Road (situated outside the city walls near to Walmgate Bar). Whilst some sources suggest that traffic was first carried over the line in December 1879, the official opening date is quoted as 1 January 1880. Over the years the line was quite busy: it carried coal for both the local gas works and the power station, livestock for the cattle market (then located in Barbican Road opposite the present day Barbican Centre), Rowntrees' and NER Laundry Siding traffic,

Nestlé-Rowntree) – announced their intention to cease using rail transport as from April 1987. This disastrous turn of events was prompted, it was said, by a deterioration of the internal rail network within the Haxby Road factory, and they also claimed that the investment needed to update the system could not be financially justified. (Shortly afterwards a fleet of new 38 Tonne lorries appeared on the scene.) A complete reappraisal of the whole situation freightwise concluded

that Speedlink operations would henceforth be centred upon Doncaster, and the by now inevitable closure of Dringhouses Yard soon followed. Such residual freight activities as are left at York were thereafter dealt with at York Yard North and in the Up Yard, though it is gratifying to note that quite a considerable number of freight trains can still be seen at York – particularly MGR coal trains – and an account of the current freight operations scene appears in Chapter 9.

together with transfers exchanged to and from the Derwent Valley Light Railway which opened in 1913.

The branch was a single line, apart from a short section of double track at the Burton Lane end, and a modified form of Staff & Ticket working was in operation under the control of the Burton Lane signalman and the Foss Islands shunter (designated 'Staff Attendant' in the old Appendices). A simple one platform halt was opened in November 1927 right outside Rowntrees' factory for the benefit of employees and parties of invited visitors, though patronage eventually fell away leading to its closure from 8 July 1988. Original-

ly called 'Rowntrees' Cocoa Works', the halt was situated on its own separate loop line alongside the double track portion of the Foss Islands branch end and as will be noted from the accompanying sketch, outgoing passenger or empty stock trains had to run on to the down Scarborough line at Burton Lane box in order to gain access to the up line towards York.

Rowntrees factory was served by a private siding (Agreement dated 17 February 1891); the internal railway system being reached via a steeply inclined connection from a ground frame released by the Burton Lane signalman. Prior to the loss of the sundries traffic in 1971, it was

usual to see three trips per day operating out of Rowntrees' siding, but latterly this came down to two, and, as explained earlier, the whole of the traffic was lost from rail to road in April 1987. Developments such as North Sea gas and the big Aire Valley power stations meant that coal traffic ceased to pass by rail to the local gas works and power station, but on the

Below:
York Foss Islands Goods Yard.
Author's Collection

Bottom:
Burton Lane Box — facsimile of box diagram. *Author's Collection*

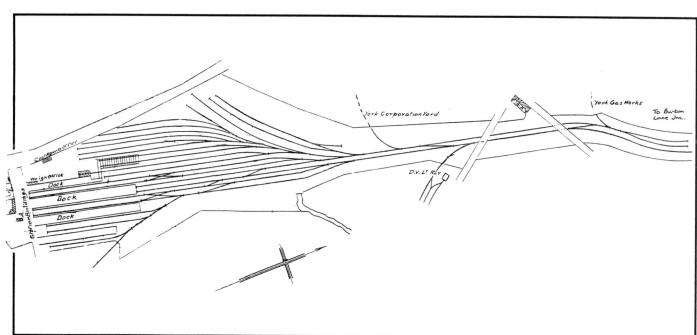

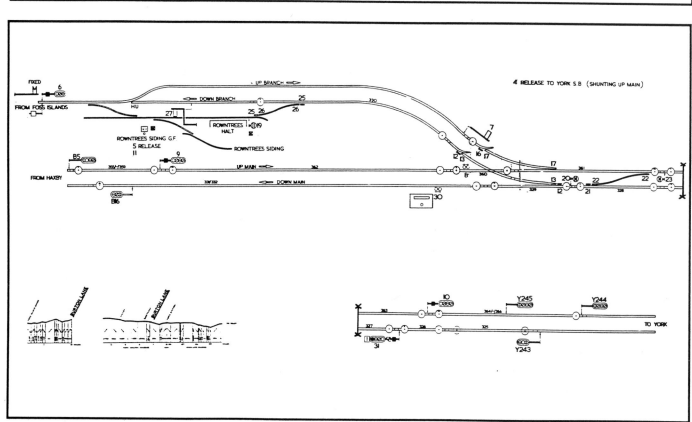

Right:
A RCTS rail-tour on 20 June 1954 has traversed the Derwent Valley Light Railway and is heading for York station along the Foss Islands branch. It has just passed under Heworth Green and is alongside the former NER Laundry, with wagons of coal for the boilers in the Laundry siding. The train is hauled by Class J21 0-6-0 No 65078. *C. Ord*

Below:
Class 08 No 08062, with a Rowntrees-Dringhouses trip working, passes Platform 4 (8B) at York station on 14 April 1984. The wagons were part of a specially insulated VDA fleet constructed for the transport of chocolate and confectionery manufactured at the Haxby Road factory. The factory possessed a private siding connected to the Foss Islands branch. *M. J. Collins*

other hand, the closure of Leeman Road coal depots in 1966 increased the domestic coal activity at Foss Islands.

Moreover, the transfer of full loads traffic from Leeman Road goods station in 1972 concentrated the remaining freight handling facilities at Foss Islands. The livestock traffic dwindled away towards the end of the 1970s, (and in any case the cattle market was relocated to a new non-rail connected site at Murton outside the city altogether), and by the early 1980s the main traffic dealt with was sand and limestone for Messrs

Redfearn's National Glass. When National Glass eventually decided to concentrate activities upon their Monk Bretton works (near Barnsley), the future outlook for the Foss Islands branch began to look very bleak indeed and the loss of the Rowntrees' traffic sealed its fate completely. By then, the Derwent Valley Railway had closed, except for occasional movements of oil traffic to a depot on DVR territory at Layerthorpe (see Chapter 11), the contract for which expired during October 1988, and in any case Foss Islands had

been closed as a public freight depot from 6 August 1984. The branch and its various sidings have since been lifted, and a large DIY complex now occupies the former Foss Islands goods yard site.

At the time of writing (in September 1992), proposals are being developed by the Sustrans organisation (who specialise in these matters) to convert the abandoned track-bed of the branch into a cycle path between Wigginton Road (near the site of Rowntrees' Halt) and Osbaldwick (which was on the former Derwent Valley line).

5. Motive Power Depots and Workshops

Some 60-70 years ago, in the heyday of steam, there were engine sheds to be seen on both sides of the line at the south end of York station. The shed on the up side accommodated 'foreign' visitors to York until 1933, whilst York's own allocation of smaller locomotives occupied the three (latterly two) roundhouses on the down side. North of the station – on the down side – one could always observe a wide variety of locomotives around the yard at the North shed, and a lot of activity always seemed to be taking place.

The South Sheds

The Y&NM workshops to maintain their locomotives were built on the south side of the line adjacent to the first temporary terminus situated just outside the city walls. (One of these workshop buildings, now demolished, housed the old Railway Museum.) Additionally, the Y&NM straight shed was built on the north side of the line on a site now occupied by Platform 7 (11); subsequently it was demolished to make way for the 1877 station.

In the triangle between the Holgate Junction-North Junction (York Yard South) line and the original GNE route giving access to the 1841 station, five further sheds were built – three roundhouses (or circular sheds) and two straight sheds. The first two circular sheds dated from 1851 and 1852 respectively; each had 16 stalls served by a 42ft turntable. It is not known when the first shed went out of use for locomotive purposes, though prior to the Grouping it was being used for the repair of wagon sheets. Later a NER petrol-engined saloon was kept there; however, the building was destroyed by a fire during the night of 21/22 October 1921 and afterwards demolished. The second shed remained in use until May 1961, when the practice of stabling pilots at the South shed ceased, although surplus locomotives were stored there for some time prior to its demolition during November 1963.

A third roundhouse, larger than the other two, was built during 1864; it had a 45ft turntable and 18 stalls, each with a separate ribbed roof. This shed also

Below:
The oldest engine shed at York was the three-road straight shed at the south end of the station, originating in 1841, probably for the Great North of England Railway. For a time it was occupied by the Great Northern engines stationed at York, and in the 1930s by the LMS engines, such as '3P' 4-4-0 No 731. It was demolished in November 1963. The small coaling stage on the right was used to refuel the 'J71' and 'J72' pilot engines *L. W. Perkins*

Left:
York (South) sidings behind Locomotive Yard box: a mid-1930s shot of NER Class R (LNER Class D20) No 1234. The locomotive was built in 1907 and withdrawn in May 1943. *Author's Collection*

Below left:
T. W. Worsdell 0-6-0T No 1197 (LNER Class J71) was built in 1892 and withdrawn in November 1956. It is seen, possibly prewar, at York (South). Note the enormous length of Locomotive Yard box (rear view) in the background. *Author's Collection*

Below:
York (North) sheds in the mid-1930s – now the NRM site – with Raven Atlantic Class Z (LNER Class C7) No 2172 on a down express. *Author's Collection*

alterations were carried out at the south end of York station. Previously the boiler shop of the then York Locomotive Works (which closed in 1905), Queen Street shed went out of use after 1933, and in more recent years inspection saloons were stored there until its demolition in 1974.

The North Sheds

In conjunction with the 1877 layout alterations, authorisation was given on 5 November 1875 for the construction of a shed to hold 60 locomotives at 'Clifton', situated on the west side of the line north of the new station. The 'North' shed as it became known, opened early in 1878, comprising three integral roundhouses with 20 roads and a 45ft turntable, together with a coal stage. In 1891, the original 45ft turntable in No 2 shed was replaced by a 50ft model, and in 1911 two

closed in May 1961 and was demolished during November 1963. Of the two straight sheds at the south end, one apparently was the GNE three road shed, opened in 1841 and demolished in 1963. Although the GNE shed was almost identical in style to another shed at Darlington – which still stands adjacent to the erstwhile S&D crossing, though no longer in railway use – the York building had its roof renewed in an altogether different style during the 1930s. The other straight shed, of unknown origin, was latterly used as a 'Signal Fitting' shop until its demolition in 1936/37 in connection with the layout alterations which preceded the construction of new Platforms 10/11 (15/16). This particular shed stood in a position almost parallel with the original GNE line leading to and from the 'old' station, and in the 1909 layout alterations the building had one corner cut off to give more space beyond Platform 9 (14). The shed on the up side of the line was known as 'Queen Street'; it was a four road straight shed which opened in 1909, at the same time as the extensions and

new electric turntables were ordered – the first to replace the 45ft one in No 3 shed; the other to be used in the proposed new No 4 shed which was also authorised in 1911. A new coal stage and many other improved facilities were provided in order to modernise what had become one of the NER's principal motive power depots, and the work was finally completed in 1915. The new No 4 shed was built on to the north end of the existing building.

After the 1923 Grouping, the LNER embarked upon a number of schemes to improve motive power depot facilities all over the system. York acquired an electrically operated 70ft turntable of the 'Mundt' non-balancing type supplied by Ransome Rapier Ltd in 1932, and at the same time a mechanical coaling plant was installed. To move on a few years, disaster struck in the early hours of 29 April 1942, during the same air-raid which devastated York station; the shed suffered a direct hit which caused such extensive damage to a couple of locomotives that they both had to be written off and withdrawn from service. The two locomotives were 'B16' 4-6-0 No 925 and 'A4' 4-6-2 No 4469 *Sir Ralph Wedgwood* (originally called *Gadwall* until renamed in March 1939). The name *Sir Ralph Wedgwood* was subsequently carried by another Class A4 locomotive No 4466 *Herring Gull,* so renamed in January 1944 and ran until withdrawal in 1965. Half a century later, on 29 April 1992, a commemorative plaque was unveiled on the floor of the NRM Great Hall on the exact spot where the bomb fell in the then running shed destroying the two locomotives.

Top right:
Pump House sidings, on the up side of the ECML, immediately north of Waterworks Crossing with 'C7' Atlantic No 2211 during the mid-1920s. (Note LNER and engine number on tender gives some indication of period.) The signal gantry in the background applied to the Up Scarborough branch, and Scarborough Bridge is just visible below the engine's buffer beam. *Author's Collection*

Centre right:
A vintage NER 2-4-0 dating from 1885 and rebuilt in 1893, (LNER Class E5). This locomotive was withdrawn in 1928 and it is standing in what is now part of the NRM Great Hall. *Author's Collection*

Right:
NER Class 190 2-2-4T No 1679 rebuilt 1894 and withdrawn (LNER Class X3) in June 1931. The date of the photograph is unknown but the location is now within the present-day Great Hall of the NRM. The pristine condition suggests use on the Board of Directors inspection saloon trips, and it is worthy of note that No 1679 hauled the inaugural train from Layerthorpe to Cliff Common on the occasion of the DVLR opening ceremony on 19 July 1913. *Author's Collection*

Left:
A scene of absolute desolation at York North MPD taken on the morning of Wednesday 29 April 1942, just a few hours after the disastrous air-raid. The severely damaged 'A4' *Sir Ralph Wedgwood* and its tender can be seen in the centre of the picture. It is rather difficult to imagine that the NRM Great Hall now stands on this site! *BR*

Below left:
A 'grand finale' of Deltics outside York MPD on 5 November 1981, a short while before the last remaining survivors were withdrawn from traffic. *BR*

During the 1950s a rebuilding programme was undertaken, and in 1954 the 70ft turntable in No 4 shed was replaced. Finally, during 1957/58, Nos 1 and 2 roundhouses were demolished and replaced by a straight shed/repair shop, whilst Nos 3 and 4 sheds were rebuilt and re-roofed as two roundhouses retaining their turntables and radiating stalls. (Nos 3 and 4 sheds now form an integral part of the National Railway Museum.)

It is interesting to note that in December 1923, York's total locomotive allocation was 150. By the end of 1932 this figure had risen to 165, and during the peak of World War 2 additional traffic, York had an all time high total of 178 locomotives on its books in March 1943. Even in January 1964, the total allocation was 166 (94 steam and 72 diesel), but by January 1971 this figure had been reduced to 64 diesels.

The last steam locomotives were transferred away from York on 25 June 1967, and in 1970 the coaling plant was demolished (with great difficulty!), followed in 1973 by the demolition of the 100,000 gallon water tank (which dated from 1909).

Ultimately, York's role as an important motive power depot declined to the point where its remaining allocation of main line diesel locomotives, by then down to a total of 37, was transferred away in January 1982 leaving only a handful of diesel shunting locomotives based there.

Nevertheless, in the final years following the demise of steam, York depot was destined to become the home for the majority of the 22-strong 'Deltic' fleet (all but three actually), as will be seen in Chapter 8.

Disposition of Other Companies' Locomotives at York

Over the years, facilities were provided for what both the NER and LNER regarded as 'foreign companies' locomotives, and as the story is somewhat complicated, it will be recounted in chronological order. Great Northern

locomotives were outbased at York from 1850, and following the inception of the NER in 1854 they were accommodated in the former GNE straight shed at York (South) until the Grouping; afterwards they were moved to the North shed. Midland locomotives came next after the S&K Joint line opened in 1879, and they were given use of the 1864 roundhouse up to the Grouping. After the Grouping, when the LMS company was formed, the ex-Midland locomotives were moved across to Queen Street to join those of the ex-L&Y Railway. The L&Y outbased locomotives, together with those of the GE and GC companies, had been accommodated in one of the York (South) roundhouses until 1909, when they moved over to the then newly rehabilitated Queen Street shed, though after the Grouping the former GE and GC locomotives had become LNER property and were transferred elsewhere. LMS locomotives had exclusive use of Queen Street shed until its closure in 1933, when they were again moved back across the line – this time into the ex-GNE straight shed previously vacated by those of the GN 10 years earlier.

After Nationalisation in 1948, most locomotives were dealt with at the main North shed, and use of York (South) sheds gradually declined until closure in 1961. By this time, the south sheds had become structurally unsound, and their inevitable demolition followed in 1963.

LNER Class A2 Raven Pacific 4-6-2 No 2402 *City of York*

The relatively short-lived Raven Pacifics are worth a mention as one of the class was named *City of York*. These were the last new locomotives to be designed by Sir Vincent Raven, who had been the NER's Chief Mechanical Engineer since 1910. Essentially an elongated version of his successful 4-4-2 Class Z Atlantics, it seems probable that Raven was trying to steal a march on Gresley whose Pacifics in the event proved to be infinitely superior in all respects. On 30 March 1922, Darlington Works received authority to build two new Pacifics, and although both locomotives of the original order were nominally completed in time to be

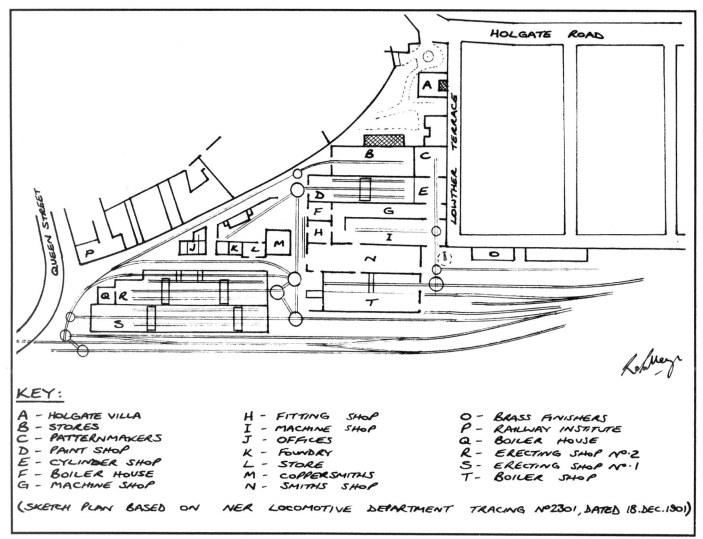

KEY:

A – HOLGATE VILLA
B – STORES
C – PATTERNMAKERS
D – PAINT SHOP
E – CYLINDER SHOP
F – BOILER HOUSE
G – MACHINE SHOP

H – FITTING SHOP
I – MACHINE SHOP
J – OFFICES
K – FOUNDRY
L – STORE
M – COPPERSMITHS
N – SMITHS SHOP

O – BRASS FINISHERS
P – RAILWAY INSTITUTE
Q – BOILER HOUSE
R – ERECTING SHOP Nº 2
S – ERECTING SHOP Nº 1
T – BOILER SHOP

(SKETCH PLAN BASED ON NER LOCOMOTIVE DEPARTMENT TRACING Nº 2301, DATED 18.DEC.1901)

Above:
NER Locomotive Works Queen Street York (1901). *R. D. Pulleyn*

regarded as 'North Eastern' stock, they did not enter traffic until early 1923. Under LNER auspices a further three examples of this type were built in 1924, and a decision was taken to name them after cities located in ex-NER territory.

No 2402, the first of the 1924 batch, became *City of York* and to the best of the author's knowledge, was the only steam locomotive to bear this name. Initially allocated to Gateshead depot, the whole class was transferred to York during 1934. No 2402 came to York shed on 13 August 1934 where it remained at work for the rest of its short life until withdrawal from service on 25 July 1936. Actually, the 'Raven' Pacifics were the first examples of LNER built locomotives to be scrapped after the grouping, as the following details show:

Workshops: 1 Queen Street

In March 1842, the Y&NM invited tenders for the construction of workshops, and in 1844 further tenders were sought so as to make adequate provision for the maintenance of the company's rapidly growing fleet of locomotives and rolling stock. The site chosen was outside the city walls quite near to where the first temporary station had been in 1839, and by 1865 the area was occupied by a variety of buildings, mostly situated on the east side of the then main line from the 'old' station to the south, though the 'engine houses' (as they were called in those days) were built on the west side. York never really became a centre for locomotive building; virtually all new locomotives were built by contractors, though a lot of rebuilding was done to bring the old stock up to date. Interestingly, No 1438, one of a batch of NER 'BTP' class rebuilt at York as a 0-6-0T

between 1899 and 1904, survived well into BR days as No 64808, and, when withdrawn in February 1961, was the last Class J77 in service.

One of the buildings was a wagon shop (which became redundant upon the opening of the new Wagon Works in 1867), so it was replaced by a Locomotive Erecting Shop together with a similar structure later built alongside. However, the accommodation at Queen Street was cramped, to say the least, and left little or no room for expansion. In addition, the NER was in dispute with the local authority regarding the rates, and as a large new erecting shop had been completed at Darlington North Road Works

Top right:
Raven Pacific No 2402 *City of York* in the mid-1920s at the Pump House sidings (opposite side of the main line from North Sheds). Note Scarborough Bridge and faint image of York Minster in the background. *Author's Collection*

Right:
Raven Pacific No 2403 *City of Durham* is pictured near the 1915 coaling stage at York North sheds. A new mechanical coaling plant was installed in 1932; it was demolished in 1970. *C. Ord*

No	Built	Name	Transferred	Withdrawn
2400	Dec 1922	*City of Newcastle*	7 May 1934	Apr 1937
2401	Dec 1922	*City of Kingston upon Hull*	9 Feb 1934	Jul 1936
2402	Mar 1924	*City of York*	13 Aug 1934	25 Jul 1936
2403	Mar 1924	*City of Durham*	26 Apr 1934	May 1937
2404	Mar 1924	*City of Ripon**	7 Nov 1934	Feb 1937

* No 2404 reboilered September 1929 with Gresley Class A1 type boiler.

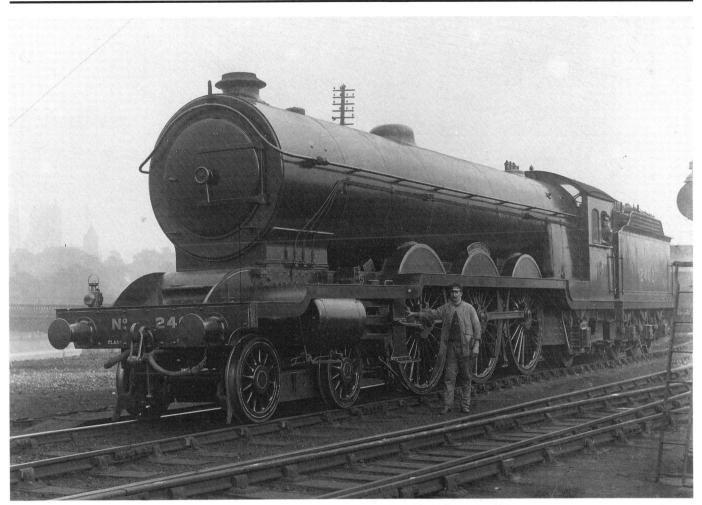

Right:
Raven Pacific No 2404 *City of Ripon*, which was reboilered in 1929 (hence the slightly different appearance), is caught in the mid-1930s at the sidings outside York MPD. *C. Ord*

in 1903, it was decided to close down the York locomotive workshops operation and transfer the activities to Darlington.

This took effect in 1905 and over the years the buildings were adapted for other railway purposes. For example, in 1907, some buildings were taken over by the then expanding Road Motors Department; the erecting shop, nearest the present day car park, became a carriage shed and subsequently an Unclaimed Goods Depot, and the erecting shop nearest to the Railway Institute was converted into a gymnasium and sports centre, being formally handed over to the Institute on 10 February 1926.

Then during the 1920s the two fitting/machine shops were used to house the various exhibits which were destined to form the nucleus of the old railway museum which opened in 1928. The former boiler shop was mentioned earlier in this chapter as becoming a shed for the accommodation of 'foreign' locomotives in 1909. This assortment of buildings was to be found in the area of the present day Railway Institute (which opened on 4 July 1889), though some of them have since been demolished – such as the old museum premises which disappeared during April 1979, the site now being used as a car park.

Workshops: 2 The Wagon Works

In 1865, the NER decided that a need existed for a new wagon works to replace the outmoded facilities at Queen Street, which by this time had no potential for expansion. A completely different site was chosen to the east of North Junction (York Yard South in present day language), and the new premises opened in 1867. Eventually, as the Wagon Works expanded, the site covered an area of some 17 acres, of which 4½ acres were occupied by buildings. The most modern building was a lifting shop built on the site of the sawmill which was destroyed by fire in 1931. However, the strategy adopted by the LNER after the Grouping

Left:
In this fascinating aerial view of the Holgate Road Carriage Works (latterly BREL – now ABB Transportation Ltd!), probably taken during the 1950s, there is an extensive panorama of the traditional York Yards area. Obviously prior to the 1958/59 Up Yard remodelling, one can see No 1 and No 2 Down Yards adjacent to the Carriage Works, and also No 1 and No 2 Up Yards to the right thereof. The 1877 ECML is visible further right with a down passenger train approaching the 'Severus Curve'. *BR*

proved to be different from that of the NER, in that the LNER concentrated new builds upon the recently opened wagon works at Faverdale (at Darlington – opened in 1923), and the long established wagon works at Shildon, leaving York to deal with overhaul and repairs. Moving forward through the 'Beeching' era of the 1960s, and the consequential reduction in the wagon fleet occurring around that time, a separate Workshops Division of British Rail had been formed following the 1962 Transport Act. A far reaching examination of workshops' activities concluded that surplus capacity existed on the wagon building and repair side, and arising from this review, York Wagon Works was closed in 1965. (Faverdale, the newest wagon works in the Northeast, closed in 1963, though Shildon managed to survive until 1984.)

Notwithstanding closure in 1965, York Wagon Works lived to fight another day and continued to repair wagons – albeit on a reduced scale – for another 20 years or so. Also, part of the premises was taken over by the neighbouring Carriage Works for use as a Test House for new builds of modern coaching stock. At the present time, the Wagon Works site is used by Trainload Freight's Fleet Engineer for the maintenance and repair of railway departmental wagons etc.

Workshops: 3 The Carriage Works

Located on the west side of the former GNE main line between North Junction and Severus, (or York Yard South and York Yard North to use today's names), the earliest known date of a contract for erection of the Holgate Road Carriage Works is 9 September 1880. Further new buildings were authorised in 1882/83, and the Carriage Works was established on its present site in 1884. By 1910, the premises had extended to cover a total area of 45 acres, 13 of which were occupied by buildings. After 1884, the new works took on the task of building and maintaining the whole of the NER's

coaching stock fleet, and from 1895 it built many of the East Coast Joint Stock (ECJS) vehicles. Furthermore, York Works built the electric stock (in later years to become its speciality) for the 1904 North Tyneside suburban electrification scheme.

After the Grouping in 1923, the whole of the LNER (NE Area) coaching stock fleet became York's responsibility, and new construction of vehicles to Gresley design was also undertaken. During both World Wars, York Works played an important part in carrying out government contracts, and manufactured a wide variety of items – not always connected with railways! During World War 2, on 15 December 1944, the works suffered a major disaster when the main Carriage Building Shop was completely destroyed by fire, though remarkably this was soon replaced by a new shop specially designed and equipped for the progressive construction of new vehicles – a technique pioneered by Mr A. H. Peppercorn, a one time Works Manager at York during the 1930s. Work continued on traditional coaching stock designs until the mid-1950s, after which York tended to specialise, from 1958 onwards, in the construction of electrical multiple-units (EMUs). Extensive modernisation of the works was carried out between 1965 and 1967, under the auspices of the then BR Workshops Division, but before long yet another reorganisation took place which was to radically change the whole situation.

Workshops: 4 The BREL Period

Just as the 1962 Transport Act had created a Workshops Division of BR, the 1968 Transport Act established British Rail Engineering Limited (BREL) as a wholly owned subsidiary of BR. BREL commenced trading in its own right from 1 January 1970, and thereafter BR assumed the role of a holding company, for want of a better description. York continued to receive plenty of work from BR and were also allowed to seek orders from outside. Hence, just to quote two examples, orders were obtained to build new vehicles for Taiwan and the Northern Ireland Railways.

Everything ran smoothly for a few years, then the commercial environment was radically altered during the mid-1980s and BR was obliged to invite competitive tendering for procurement of new rolling stock. Also, during 1985/86 significant changes took place within the workshops organisation, thus York Works became part of a separate construction business along with two other works at Derby and one at Crewe. Then in November 1987, along came the

Below:
The North Eastern was well known for its Bain clerestory coaches, such as this Brake Third built at York in 1896. *BR*

Bottom:
From 1895 York Carriage Works built vehicles for the East Coast Joint Stock fleet, such as this 56ft 6in 10-berth sleeping car turned out in 1906 and condemned in 1931. The fish-bellied underframe was favoured by the NER, but it was replaced by a normal frame in the 1920s. *L. Ward Collection*

announcement made by the then Transport Secretary, Mr Paul Channon, that BREL was to be privatised. This privatisation meant that York, along with Crewe and the two Derby Works were to be sold as a single unit, and a further announcement made at the end of 1988 confirmed the sale to a consortium mainly dominated by Asea Brown-Boveri (Sweden/Switzerland) and Trafalgar House (UK). Completion date was 18 April 1989, and thereafter the company traded under the name BREL Limited. Following a series of one crisis after another, when even the threat of closure was apparent, Trafalgar House eventually sold their holding in BREL Ltd to Asea Brown-Boveri who then held a 80% stake in the company. Then almost immediately afterwards, the Annual Report for 1991 revealed a pre-tax loss of £43 million, and the future looked decidedly grim.

Some good news was the placement of a substantial order for the construction of 188 Class 465 'Networker' EMUs for Network SouthEast, announced on 10 April 1992, which brought welcome relief to the situation, and it was hoped that the fortunes of York Works might

have taken a turn for the better. In fact, according to the local evening newspaper, the present management of Asea Brown-Boveri went on record as having expressed confidence in the future prospects of BREL Ltd, and they were of the view that full membership of the ABB Group would help to strengthen its position in both UK and overseas markets.

However, since these somewhat optimistic forecasts, another unknown factor has arisen – namely the latest Government proposals for the privatisation of British Rail – and while it is early days yet to predict the outcome of these latest developments, one cannot escape from wondering whether the future of York's Carriage Works has once again had a shadow of doubt cast upon it? Finally, the title 'BREL' recently passed into oblivion. On Wednesday 2 September 1992 the corporate name was changed to 'ABB Transportation Ltd', doubtless to reflect the fact that the parent group Asea Brown-Boveri now own the majority shareholding, (and perhaps the ABB group are seeking to distance themselves from any implied or perceived connection with BR?).

6. Signalling at York up to the 1960s

Pre-1877 Signalling Arrangements

Signalling arrangements in the early days of railways often proved to be primitive in the extreme, and the haphazard methods of working frequently attracted criticism from the Board of Trade's Inspecting Officers whenever they reported upon their accident investigations. For instance, following a collision on the curve between North Junction and Holgate Junction, (between a passenger train and some freight wagons detached during a shunting movement), on 21 August 1857, Lt-Col Geo Wynne commented in his report that 'The curve is so great between the junctions, that the signals of one cannot be seen by the other; and, therefore, when a train enters the (old) station by one junction, the signalman there rings a bell at the other junction, to warn the signalman that he is shortly to expect a train by the other junction, and to act accordingly'. The Inspecting Officer continued 'and this is the only signalling that takes place between the two junctions'. He concluded his report by saying that the methods of signalling were, in his opinion, 'defective', and called for some more efficient arrangements to be made.

Ten years later, on 9 April 1867, another collision occurred on this curve, due this time to a misunderstanding during some shunting operations, and Maj C. S. Hutchinson who took the enquiry made similar observations.

Another mishap, on 25 November 1871, when a passenger train being propelled from Holgate Bridge Junction towards the 'old' station was inadvertently diverted into the 'Coke Siding' (due to yet another misunderstanding!), brought forth the comment from Col W. Yolland that 'the points are not all worked from the signal box and properly interlocked with the signals and with each other'. This time, the report concluded with the remark 'The Company have powers to erect a new station at

York, and I trust that when it is constructed these objectionable arrangements will be done away with'.

Then again, reporting upon a collision in the 'old' station, which occurred on 12 August 1872, Capt H. W. Tyler remarked 'There is a signal cabin close to the archway, and the signalman there stationed controls the approach to various lines in the station; and he uses his fixed signals and his hand signals according to circumstances'. This time it seems that Capt Tyler almost 'threw in the towel' in dismay, for he concluded by saying 'I cannot blame any of the men in this case. The only wonder is that they are able to work the traffic as they do without accidents constantly occurring'.

In fairness to the old North Eastern Railway, the company was very active during the 1870s by introducing both the block telegraph system and interlocking of points with signals. Actually, the NER had made a conscious decision to equip their principal routes before they were forced to do so by legislation, for the Regulation of Railways Act 1889 made the adoption of the block system on passenger lines compulsory by law. The same parliamentary act also specified continuous brakes, and concentration of points and signals operation into lever frames with full interlocking as mandatory requirements for passenger carrying railways.

In another report upon a collision which took place on 15 September 1872 (when a passenger train ran into the rear of a slow moving freight train) between Copmanthorpe and 'Chandlers Whin', Capt Tyler acknowledged that block working was then in force, but he placed great stress upon the lack of interlocking between the distant and home signal at Copmanthorpe. (The distant signal was 'off' – ie, clear, on this particular occasion, with the home and advance signals in the 'on' – ie danger position!)

And, yet another mishap, which happened on 20 December 1872 involving a collision between a departing passenger

train and a GN light engine near North Junction. This prompted Lt-Col C. S. Hutchinson to say '(there is) telegraphic bell communication between the station (Archway) and the junction (North Jct) cabins for announcing the arrival and departure of trains'. He concluded with a remark that 'the recurrence of a similar collision might be avoided by no passenger train being allowed to leave the station until the line is clear up to the junction', and he went on to recommend the provision of a distant signal.

Prior to the major track layout alterations effected during 1877, which culminated in the 'new' (ie, present) York station being opened on 25 June of that year, numerous signal cabins had been provided as the development of block working and interlocking proceeded from around 1870 onwards. (Note the term 'signal cabin' was then in general use throughout NER territory and in contemporary official publications, whereas the more modern version 'signal box' first appeared in the 1898 Appendix.)

On the former Y&NM line, proceeding southwards from the 'old' station, there were signal cabins at Archway, Locomotive Yard (the first of three cabins to bear that name), South Ticket Platform, Middle and Holgate Bridge Junction in that order. Then followed Excursion Platform, South Points, North Lane, and, from 1870 'Chandlers Whin' where a junction was made with the newly constructed direct main line to Doncaster via Selby opened to traffic on 2 January 1871. The last two cabins were situated at level crossings adjacent to the present day road overbridges at St Helens Road and Moor Lane respectively.

On the former GNE line going north, the signal cabins were (from the junction with the former Y&NM line controlled by Archway), South View, North Junction, Holgate Beck, New Goods Yard, Gas Works and Poppleton Junction.

In 1877, concurrently with the 'new'

station being opened, the double track going southwards was widened to provide four roads as far as 'Chandlers Whin' where the junction with the then comparatively new main line towards Selby was removed, and the cabin dispensed with. In practice, outgoing trains from York were routed on to their proper tracks from Locomotive Yard or Holgate Bridge cabins, and at the site of the former 'Chandlers Whin' junction, the Selby line veered away to the left, whereas the Leeds/Normanton line (double track only in those days) carried straight on heading for Copmanthorpe and Church Fenton. Also, as a matter of interest, a second Holgate Bridge was constructed at this time, capable of spanning six tracks, because the first bridge built by the Y&NM in 1839 only carried the road over a double tracked railway.

New Signalling Arrangements 1877

Completely new signalling – quite 'modern' for its time – was required to control the extensively remodelled track layout in and around the present station. The station itself was controlled originally by three cabins: Waterworks at the north end; Platform in the centre of the station; and, Locomotive Yard (the second cabin to bear this name) at the south end. A new cabin was also provided at Holgate Bridge Junction; this was a very tall structure so that the signalmen could see along the tracks south of the road overbridge. New cabins also appeared at South Points and Clifton, thus the sequence reading from south to north after 25 June 1877 was: North Lane, South Points, Holgate Bridge Jct, Locomotive Yard, Platform, Waterworks, Clifton, Poppleton Jct and Skelton Bridge. Between Holgate Bridge and Poppleton Jct via the original GNE route (or through York Yards in today's language), there were cabins at North Jct, Holgate Beck and Severus; also, South View was still there on the former Scarborough line between North Jct and Waterworks.

Signalling Arrangements Post-1877 to the Grouping in 1923

During the 1880s a 'break-section' cabin called Askham Bog appeared between North Lane and Copmanthorpe (it disappeared after the 1904 widening scheme), and in the early 1890s arising from the construction of the York Marshalling Yards, cabins bearing the names Nos 1 and 2 Down Goods, together with Nos 1, 2 and 3 Up Goods came into being. These were situated within the yard complex between North Junction and Severus; No 2 Down Goods had gone by the time a new NER Appendix was published in 1904, and No 3 Up Goods did not appear in a re-issued Appendix published in 1911. On the Scarborough line a short distance out of York, a new cabin by the name of Burton Lane was brought into use in 1878 in readiness for the Foss Islands branch, then still under construction, and a replacement cabin called Bootham Junction appeared in 1890. Bootham worked the gates at Wigginton Road level crossing, and until the building of a new road bridge in 1933 (Crichton Avenue), there was also a level crossing at Burton Lane.

The first of the really significant alterations affecting York station took place around the turn of the century, for in 1900 the temporary Platform 14 was opened, together with a new signal box

Below:
The up 'Flying Scotsman' hauled by 'A3' Pacific No 2575 *Galopin* **passing the 'old' Waterworks box at the north end of York station, and, rather unusually, routed towards Platform 3 (8) according to the signals. In this pre-1938 scene, Leeman Road box is to the left of the picture. The single line crossing between Platform 14 and the Scarborough branch (installed in 1900) can be observed in the foreground, and the double track crossing of the 1877 goods lines between the tender and the first coach.** *Crown Copyright; NRM, York*

Right:
A view of the 'Crewe' system power frame of 133 miniature levers, which was installed at Severus box in 1903. This 'one-off' type of power frame – as far as the NER was concerned – was replaced by a large mechanical frame of 150 levers in 1922. This work necessitated the extension of the box structure at both ends. Subsequently, in 1968, the frame was cut down in size by removal of levers 1-50 and 111-150, leaving only 51-110 in use until the box – renamed York Yard North in October 1938 – was closed on 11 May 1989 under the York IECC scheme. *Crown Copyright; NRM, York*

Below right:
The interior of Locomotive Yard box in August 1909, shortly after it was opened, taken from the high lever numbers end of the frame. *Crown Copyright; NRM, York*

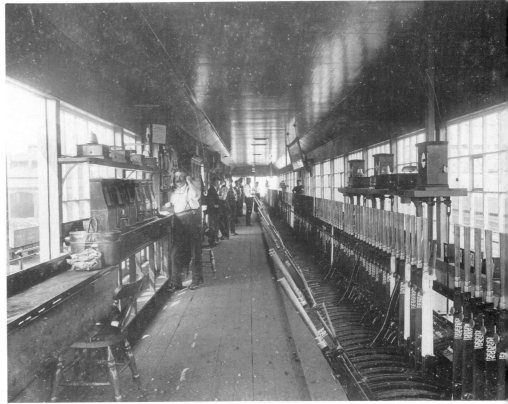

called Leeman Road situated almost opposite to Waterworks box. (The term 'box' rather than 'cabin' was then in official use.) Until the 1909 alterations at the south end of the station, the new No 14 platform was only available for use by down (northbound) ECML trains, after which it became a two-way line. Also in 1900, a completely remodelled junction at Chaloner's Whin, together with a signal box of that name, was brought into use – partly because of the new Platform 14 at York station, but also in readiness for the proposed widening from two tracks to four out as far as Church Fenton, which was started in 1900 and completed by 1904. It is of interest to note the different spellings – 'Chandlers Whin' originally, then Chaloner's Whin in 1900; though the NER adopted the Chaloner Whin version shortly afterwards, until the LNER changed it to Chaloners Whin after the Grouping.

Another development worthy of mention occurred in 1903 when the NER experimented with the 'Crewe' system of power signalling at Severus box (York Yard North from 1938). Actually, the NER was active in the development of power operated miniature lever frames and had installed some of Westinghouse manufacture in various boxes around Tyne Dock from 1902 onwards to gain experience in readiness for the major power signalling schemes which were to take place at Hull Paragon in 1904, and in the Newcastle/Gateshead localities during the 1906-1910 period.

Nevertheless, the 'Crewe' installation at Severus (supplied by the Railway Signal Co) was a 'one-off' so far as the NER was concerned, though the London & North Western (LNW) possessed several such examples at some of their boxes at Crewe. The Severus frame was a 'double decker' type containing a total of 133 miniature levers, placed alternately with the odd numbers in the upper tier and the even numbers in the lower. (For those interested in signalling, the National Railway Museum's reserve S&T collection contains an early LNWR-style power frame from Gresty Lane box, Crewe, which can be viewed by appointment.) A new box was built for this installation which was commissioned on 21 September 1903, and nearly 20 years later it was decided to revert to the old manual system, as by that time the sole example of this type of power frame on the NER was proving both difficult and expensive to maintain. Thus the 1903 structure was extended at both ends, and a mechanical frame containing 150 levers installed at the back of the box was brought into use on 9 April 1922 (subsequently shortened to 60 levers in 1968).

Without doubt, the main event of the early 20th century, in the context of York signalling, was the opening of the large third (and last) Locomotive Yard box in 1909, which contained a very long Pattern 16 frame of McKenzie & Holland

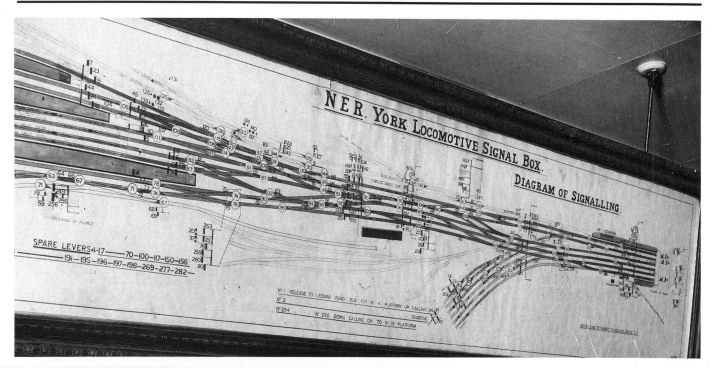

of routes. (A space was provided between levers 145 and 146 to permit easy access for the Regulator's sheltered alcove on the balcony.)

Signalling alterations also took place at the north end of the station; the principal effect being the provision of a single line connection between the then Platform 14 and the Scarborough branch, which passed to the south of Waterworks box whereas the pre-1877 Scarborough lines (by this time goods lines only) passed to the north thereof. Both Leeman Road and Waterworks boxes were involved, by means of releases and slotted signals, in movements to and from the Scarborough direction requiring to cross the main lines at the north end of York station. Furthermore, some of the 1877 signalling equipment was becoming outmoded and/or worn, thus the opportunity was taken to renew the lever frames at both Waterworks and Leeman Road boxes. Whilst the latter box was new in 1900, the scale of alterations was such that an enlarged frame of 91 levers was necessary, and Waterworks acquired two new frames numbered 1-66 and 67-132.

Other examples come to mind to illustrate how the upgrading of signalling equipment continued as an ongoing

manufacture with a total of 295 levers in one continuous row. On good authority – O. S. Nock no less – this was said to be the largest mechanical lever frame in the world. The 1909 track layout remodelling and associated resignalling was prompted by the sheer necessity to extend the station platforms for accommodating longer trains, and also to rectify a general shortage of capacity to cope adequately with the extra traffic – particularly during the summer months – at a time when railways reigned supreme over all other forms of transport. The new Locomotive Yard box was partially opened on Sunday 6 June 1909, and Hol-

gate Bridge Junction box (which had a frame of 46 levers) was closed at the same time. Then exactly one week later, on Sunday 13 June 1909, the old Locomotive Yard box (which finally had a frame of 129 levers after the 1900 alterations) was closed, and its replacement thus became fully operational. The new Locomotive Yard box was under the charge of a senior signalman, known as a Traffic Regulator, who spent most of his time out on the balcony observing the course of operations – particularly shunting movements and the numerous engine changes – and directing the 'levermen' inside the box as to the setting up

Above:
A down express is seen passing Clifton box in 1949 or 1950 hauled by Peppercorn 'A1' Pacific No 60126. This locomotive was built in 1949 and was named *Sir Vincent Raven* on 3 August 1950. It was withdrawn in January 1965. Note that when this photograph was taken the locomotive was not carrying nameplates. *J. W. Armstrong*

Below right:
South Points box, which was extended at the York end in 1915 when a new frame of 60 levers was installed. A further five levers were added in 1928 when Dringhouses box was closed. This box, along with Chaloners Whin, was closed on 8 April 1951 under Stage 1 of the York box scheme. *BR*

controlled by South Points and the exit near Holgate Bridge worked from a small signal box type of structure – which in reality was a ground frame released by Locomotive Yard box. After Holgate Bridge Junction box was closed in 1909, it had been found necessary to station a 'Lookoutman' in a small hut on the up side of the line to report the passage of down freight trains proceeding towards York Yards complete with tail lamp to enable Locomotive Yard to give 'Train out of Section' to South Points. (The pointsman at the above mentioned Holgate outlet ground frame assumed this duty until the 1951 new signalling scheme was implemented.)

Dringhouses Up Yard was also a World War 1 addition, and Dringhouses Down Yard came into being around 1918/19. A new signal box called Dringhouses, situated on the up side of the line, also opened during this same period and it was unusual in that it only signalled three of the four running lines (ie, it worked the Down Doncaster and Down Leeds lines and the Up Doncaster line but not the Up Leeds line.) Actually, Dringhouses box was located about 100yd north of the former North Lane box, which closed in 1904 after the level crossing there had been stopped up following powers obtained in 1902 which involved building a bridge to carry what is now known as St Helens Road over the railway.

The Holgate Excursion Platforms mentioned earlier were originally provided in 1860, though they were moved back in the 1877 widening scheme. Last

process. The 1877 frame of 70 levers at Platform box was replaced in 1907 by a new one of 80 levers. The structure has survived to the present day, even though it ceased to be used for signalling purposes in 1951. (It is situated on top of Messrs W. H. Smith's bookshop, and is still in use to accommodate the Duty Station Manager and Customer Care staff.) Another example of a major renewal occurred at North Junction in 1903 where a new frame of 125 levers was installed. A large replacement signal box, with a frame of 120 levers, was provided at Clifton in 1912 in connection with the extensive layout alterations at the greatly enlarged York North MPD, and the adjacent carriage sidings.

World War 1 saw the construction of additional facilities for wartime traffic at Holgate and Dringhouses, and in 1915 the box structure at South Points was extended to accommodate a new frame of 60 levers. Four additional reception lines were provided behind Holgate Down Excursion Platform, the entrance being

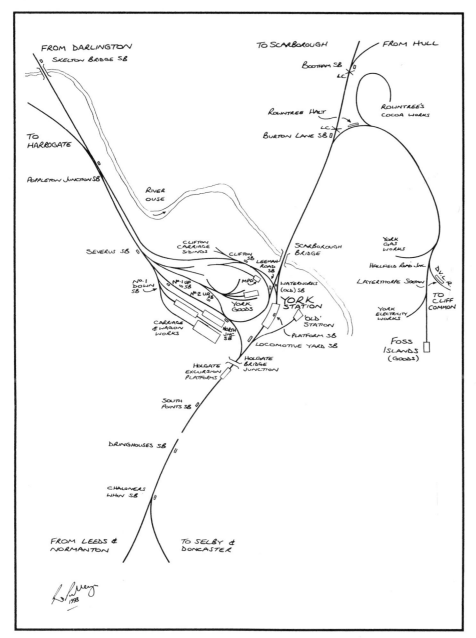

used for excursion trains in connection with York Races on 24 August 1939, these platforms were demolished in 1964. (A RCTS railtour called at the down platform to pick up passengers on 23 June 1957 – probably the very last time the platforms were used.)

Signalling Alterations 1923-1962

The relatively short lived Dringhouses box was closed on 30 September 1928 and control of the outlet from the up sidings, also the entrance to Dringhouses down receptions, was passed to South Points box which gained five extra levers in the process, increasing the frame total to 65. Apart from a few more frame renewals (such as at Chaloners Whin in 1926 when the number of levers was reduced from 110 to 80), the next important alterations occurred during the late 1930s when large scale extensions to the west side of the station were undertaken. The most significant layout alterations which affected the signalling arrangements were concerned with the construction of a new island platform beyond the then Platform 14, and a redesigned Waterworks Crossing so that only two

Left:
York Signal Boxes in 1923. North Junction became York Yard South in October 1938. Severus became York Yard North in October 1938. Poppletone Junction became Skelton in October 1938. *R. D. Pulleyn*

Below:
An up express is pictured passing Dringhouses box during the 1920s with 'A3' Pacific No 2544 *Lemberg* providing the motive power. Dringhouses box was closed on 30 September 1928, and its functions were taken over by South Points. *C. Ord*

Above:
Construction of the new island Platform 15/16 is photographed during 1938 whilst work was in progress. *BR*

Below:
A further illustration of the 1938 reconstruction shows the extension of the station footbridge from Platform 14 to the new Platforms 15/16 in progress. Note, also, the 'old' Waterworks box in the right background and Leeman Road box to the left. *BR*

tracks would cross the main lines instead of three. However, the master plan envisaged one centralised power operated signal box to control the whole of York station and the immediate locality, excluding the York Yards area. But for the outbreak of World War 2 in 1939, it is probable that York box would have opened in 1942. In the event, another nine years was to elapse before the York box scheme came to fruition.

The new No 15 platform line was

brought into use during the weekend of 2/3 April 1938, and thereafter the existing Platform 14 became an 'Engineers Construction Site' until restored to traffic a couple of months afterwards. The new No 16 platform line was worked as a bay platform connected up at the north end only. This work was followed by the opening of a 'temporary' Waterworks box (with a new frame of 110 levers positioned at the back of the box), situated slightly to the north of the 1877 structure, during the weekend of 19/20 November 1938. This expedient then permitted the demolition of the old box which stood directly in the way of the proposed new and realigned Waterworks crossing designed for access between the Scarborough branch and the then Platforms 14/15/16, plus the goods lines to and from York Yards. The so-called 'temporary' Waterworks box actually lasted for nearly 13 years due to World War 2.

Three signal boxes were renamed in October 1938; thus North Junction became York Yard South, Severus (so-called after a Roman Emperor who died at York in AD 211) became York Yard North and Poppleton Junction took the name Skelton.

The next major work occupied several days between 3/9 March 1939; this involved a radical remodelling which

Right:
A view of the York station south end
track layout and signalling taken on
20 September 1937, prior to the 1938
alterations which affected the area.
Note the South Shed roundhouse behind
Locomotive Yard box. *Ian Allan Library*

Centre right:
A similar view of the southern
approaches to York station, also taken
on 20 September 1937, this time looking
south from the end of the then
Platform 4 (later Platform 8 and now
No 3). Much of the signalling shown is as
installed in 1909. *BR*

Below:
A different view on 20 September 1937,
this time looking through Holgate
Bridge taken from the Up Excursion
Platform. The small signal box-type
structure was Holgate ground frame – a
'pointsmans' box – which was installed
in 1915 to work the outlet from Holgate
Down Receptions. Also note the LMS
locomotive – Class 2P 4-4-0 No 498. The
three signal arms facing the opposite
way on the large signal gantry were,
from left to right, South Points box's up
outer distants for the Up Leeds, Up
Doncaster and Up Excursion lines. *BR*

Right:
Another interior shot of Locomotive Yard box, this time from the low numbers end of the frame, taken on 21 August 1948. The revised signal box diagram, dating from 1938, reflects the major alterations which were made at that time. *BR*

Right:
Another interior shot of Locomotive Yard box, this time from the low numbers end of the frame, taken on 21 August 1948. The revised signal box diagram, dating from 1938, reflects the major alterations which were made at that time. *BR*

affected the north end of the then Platforms 14/15/16, together with a rearrangement of tracks between Leeman Road and Clifton boxes in order to achieve an eventual layout compatible with the long-term York resignalling plan. Also, during this period, the new Waterworks crossing was brought into full use.

During the summer of 1939, by which time it had become obvious that World War 2 was not very far off, further work was suspended on the York scheme and activity did not resume until 1946 when a start was made on converting manually worked points to power operation. Eventually, the majority of points worked from the old boxes became power operated which greatly facilitated the changeover when, at long last, York box opened in 1951.

Before describing York box in detail, the staging work is, perhaps, worthy of mention for the record. In Stage 1 which took place on Sunday 8 April 1951, Chaloners Whin and South Points boxes were closed and the 'Outer South' panel in York box was commissioned. In effect, a portion of the new box intervened between Locomotive Yard box and Naburn (Selby line) or Copmanthorpe (Church Fenton lines), and as a temporary measure between Stages 1 and 2, some bells and block instruments were provided in York box because Absolute Block working still applied on the Down Doncaster and Down Leeds lines, and Permissive Block on the Down Holgate Excursion line, going towards Locomotive Yard box from the direction of Chaloners Whin.

Stage 2 took place over two days on Sunday/Monday 20/21 May 1951 when the remaining manual boxes at York station were closed; namely Locomotive Yard, Platform, Waterworks, Leeman Road and Clifton. The new York box became fully operational at 11.59pm on Monday 20 May 1951, with the exception that the then Platforms 15/16 were not available for movements to and from the south until Stage 3 was completed the following Sunday (27 May 1951). This was because Locomotive Yard box had to be demolished, as the new connections at the south end of these platforms had to be laid across the site it occupied.

The fringe boxes which interfaced with York box were, at that time, Naburn,

Right:
Engineering work in progress outside Locomotive Yard box during 1950 in preparation for the 1951 resignalling.
E. Sanderson

Above:
This scene at Waterworks Crossing dates from 1949 or 1950. Note the re-aligned double track crossing over the main lines which was brought into use in 1939, and the 'temporary' Waterworks box of 1938. Leeman Road box is to the left of the picture. 'A3' Pacific No 60045 *Lemberg* is leaving the north end of Platform 5 (9) with a down express, and Clifton's distant signal is 'off' for a clear run to Skelton! *E. Sanderson*

Left:
A view of York station north end on 21 August 1948. Note the exterior wall of York box to the right of the picture above the roof canopy of Platform 14. *BR*

Below left:
Locomotive Yard box is seen on 20 September 1937. Note the Traffic Regulator's look-out position half way along the box frontage. *BR*

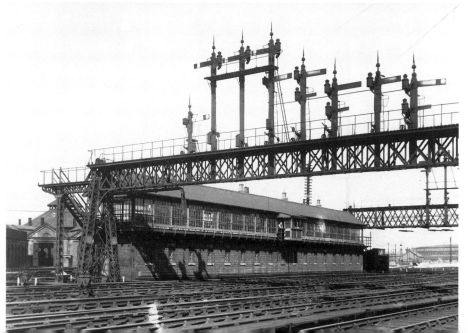

Right:
The present-day scene at Chaloners Whin on 6 August 1992 with a Class 158 DMU approaching on the Down Leeds line. The left hand pair of tracks is now the ECML as far as Colton Junction, and the name 'Chaloners Whin' has been dropped from current railway usage since it is no longer a junction.
Mrs C. A. Appleby

Left:
Chaloners Whin box on 20 September 1937 looking towards York. Opened in 1900, this box originally had a frame of 110 levers, though, when the frame was renewed in 1926, the number was reduced to 80. This box was closed on 8 April 1951 under Stage 1 of the York resignalling scheme. *BR*

Above:
Looking from Moor Lane bridge towards Chaloners Whin on 20 September 1937. The Doncaster main line of 1871 curves away to the left from the quadruple track heading south towards Church Fenton. The left hand pair of tracks are the Up and Down Normanton lines, with the Up and Down Leeds lines to the right. When the widening took place – it was opened in 1904 – new island platforms were brought into use at the three intermediate stations (Copmanthorpe, Bolton Percy and Ulleskelf) and a new station was built at Church Fenton. *BR*

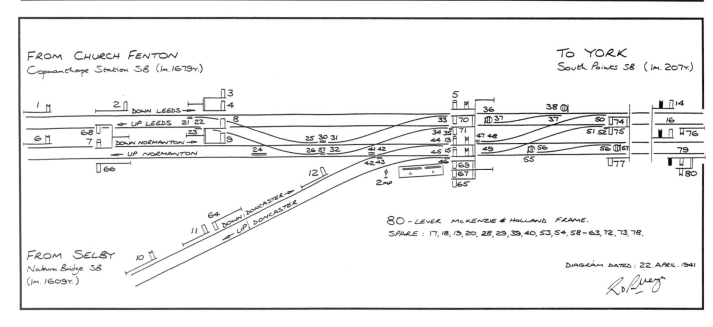

Above:
**Chaloners Whin — Track Layout &
Signalling (1941).** *R. D. Pulleyn*

Right:
York Box (1951) — Signalling.
Railway Gazette

Left:
**Locomotive Yard box on 11 May 1951
with work going ahead in preparation
for the change to electric signalling nine
days later. The box was demolished
immediately after closure to allow the
new layout to be completed the
following weekend. This work included
linking up the tracks to and from
Platforms 15/16 which are seen here
approaching the box from both
directions.** *BR*

Below:
**The classic 1951 interior shot of York
box taken shortly after full
commissioning in May of that year. At
the time it was said to be the largest
route relay interlocking in the world!**
Ian Allan Library

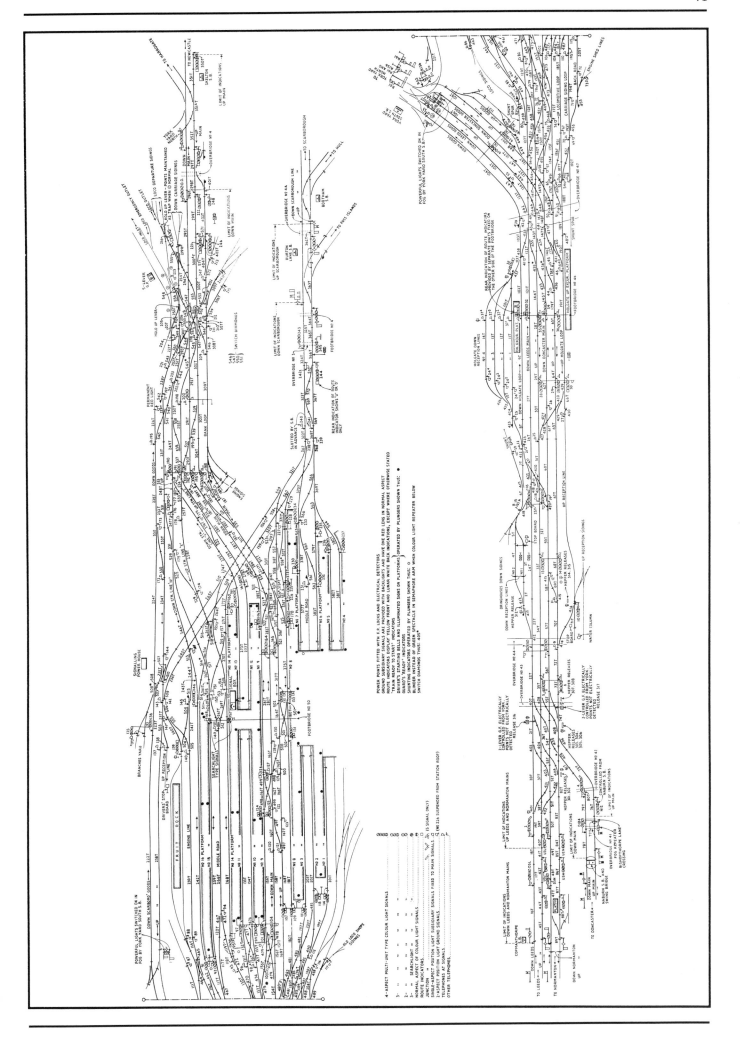

Copmanthorpe, York Yard South, Skelton and Burton Lane (or Bootham when Burton Lane was switched out of circuit, for which purpose Absolute Block working was retained on the Down Scarborough line).

York box was a Westinghouse One Control Switch (OCS) type of installation, and in a purely signal engineering context it was very much a greatly enlarged version of similarly designed power boxes at Hull Paragon (1938) and Northallerton (1939). Hull Paragon, which was the first major terminal station to be operated by a OCS route setting panel of Westinghouse design and manufacture, along with the second installation of this type at Northallerton (smaller than that at Hull but covering a larger geographical area) were the forerunners of York, which O. S. Nock described as the largest route relay interlocking in the world.

However, from a railway operating viewpoint, here, for the first time, was a large important through station and its immediate environs under the control of one central point, with all the attendant benefits of improved traffic co-ordination. Nowadays one almost takes this for granted yet it was quite a radical concept 40-odd years ago.

The new box structure was incorporated into the roof between Platforms 8 (13) and 9 (14) during the prewar extensions to the station, and for a few years following the 1942 air-raid the empty shell was used for temporary office accommodation. Upon the cessation of hostilities, work started in earnest, and as commissioned in 1951 the new installation contained 79 main colour light signals, 65 of which carried subsidiaries and 53 had route or junction indicators working with them. Additionally, there were 154

shunting signals (ground position lights – GPL – in today's language), and 277 point layouts including 15 switch 'K' crossings. The large and complicated track layout was virtually a 'like for like' resignalling of what already existed – in marked contrast to the radical simplification and remodelling which was to take place in a totally different scenario nearly 40 years later – and the 1951 box at York had a capacity for setting up 825 different routes. The four vertical indication panels were impressively large with the route setting control switches located on a sloping console immediately below and capable of being operated from a seated position. The control switches were coloured red for main routes, and white for subsidiary routes. Behind the banks of route setting switches were individual point switches, 153 in all, though these were only operated in exceptional circumstances as point operation was carried out automatically in the normal OCS sequence of route setting. The presence of trains or vehicles was indicated on the panels by means of red lights for track circuit occupation, whereas white strip lights confirmed that the routes set up by operation of the appropriate switches, had, in fact, responded correctly. Train describing was achieved by means of Standard Telephones & Cables (STC) Describers, which exhibited the details of trains by their class and intended route, rather than by the WTT reporting numbers used in more modern installations. Another feature was the two-way working (bi-directional in today's jargon) which applied on all through platforms and the through main lines in the centre of the station (except the Down Main at the north end) and proved to be of immense benefit; also the consequent

Above:
An interior shot of York Yard South box taken on 5 June 1962 to show most of the 125 lever frame installed in 1903. Note the massive STC train describers for working to and from York box. This box was closed on 29 July 1962 when the much smaller power box situated on the opposite side of the line was opened. *BR*

Left:
York Yard South's then new power box taken on 27 August 1962 to show the domino-type push-button 'Integra' panel. Note the superseded manual box in the course of demolition. *BR*

flexibility soon became evident by the improved tempo of station operations.

York box was impressive by any standards, despite being of prewar design; yet in many technical respects it was already obsolete by the day it opened – such is progress! Nevertheless, York box was destined to give many years of good service before its eventual replacement in 1989 by today's state-of-the-art technology.

Moving on to the early 1960s, an interesting piece of resignalling took place at York Yard South where the 1903 mechanical frame, and much of the signalling equipment, was life expired and in urgent need of renewal. Replacement of the frame containing 125 levers was no longer in accordance with modern sig-

describers and relay equipment was miniaturised, and it was claimed that the cost was appreciably lower than that of other contemporary installations. Whether or not this was so is open to debate, but suffice it to say that York Yard South was a 'one-off' in the then North Eastern Region. The new York Yard South box was opened on 29 July 1962, and it remained in use until displaced by the IECC on 11 May 1989.

Finally, a brief account of the ill-fated Centralised Traffic Control (CTC) scheme that never got off the ground. The plan as announced during 1960, was to single much of the York-Hull branch between Bootham and Beverley North, apart from double line stretches at either end and long passing loops at Pocklington and Market Weighton, and to introduce automation of the many intermediate minor level crossings which adversely affected the economics of this secondary route. Attendance would, of course, have been retained at certain crossings where very busy road traffic was encountered – such as at Earswick and Market Weighton West to quote a couple of examples. A new console in York box would have been provided to control this stretch of line. (The scheme was complicated by the fact that the Selby-Market Weighton-Driffield line, though proposed for closure, was still open at this time.)

However, in the event, notwithstanding the fact that materials were delivered to certain sites, this bold and pioneering experiment was doomed almost from the outset. The York-Hull direct services were withdrawn and the line between Bootham and Beverley North boxes officially regarded as closed to traffic from 29 November 1965.

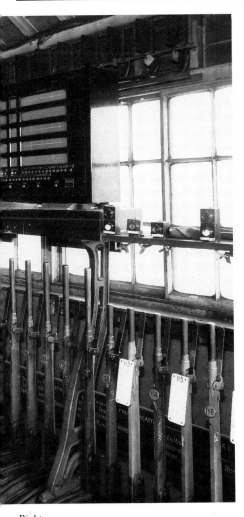

Right:
Contrast in signal box styles: (1) Copmanthorpe looking towards York on 20 September 1937. This box was situated between the Up and Down Normanton lines, quite close to the station, and opened on 12 June 1904 (in replacement of an earlier box). A short distance (c200yd) behind the photographer was Moor Lane level crossing and gate box. *BR*

Below right:
Contrast in signal box styles: (2) Copmanthorpe new box was opened on 12 November 1950. Situated at Moor Lane level crossing, both the existing gate box and the signal box at the station were closed when the new box came into use. This box lasted until 13 March 1983 when York box assumed control of the area as a prelude to the 'Selby Diversion' scheme. In this photograph, taken on 18 July 1981, the author is seen looking anxiously along the track for an approaching train! *Author's Collection*

nalling practice, and power signalling was considered to be more appropriate. A conventional power installation with route relay interlocking would have been an expensive proposition for what was essentially a 'goods' box, and eventually it was decided to try out a miniature panel of Swiss design known as 'Integra'.

Everything, including the train

7. ECML Infrastructure - A Century of Change

A century ago, the East Coast main line – both north and south of York – looked very different from today's electrified high speed railway. For instance, much of the 30-mile stretch between York and Northallerton was still only double track, supplemented by a few irregularly spaced relief sidings where slow moving freights could be backed inside and refuged to be overtaken by passenger trains. The line was signalled under the 'Block Telegraph' system which had been introduced during the 1870s, and the running of trains was controlled by some 20 signal 'cabins' with the block sections varying between a few hundred yards and up to three miles. Apart from some localised widening schemes which were undertaken around Thirsk in the mid-1870s, such as provision of an up independent goods line from Thirsk Avenue to Thirsk Middle 'cabins', together with up and down independents between Thirsk South and Green Lane, there was precious little else. Admittedly, the main line passenger service a century ago was less fast and frequent when compared with today's timetable, but the whole situation must have been an operational nightmare – especially so in attempting to regulate the seemingly endless procession of slow moving freight trains encountered in those days. In the quest to effect improvements in train performance, by increasing line capacity, a variety of widening schemes was implemented around the turn of the century, accompanied by a novel system of automatic signalling between Alne and Thirsk (Green Lane) commissioned in 1905 and known as 'Hall's Automatics'. Further major widenings, together with power signalling took place during the mid-1930s, followed by additional wartime facilities in 1942. The last widening scheme occurred as recently as 1960, thus marking completion of continuous quadruple track between Skelton Bridge and Northallerton.

South of York, the 1871 main line between the sites of the former junctions at Chaloners Whin and Barlby North

was abandoned in 1983 after being replaced by a completely new stretch of high speed railway (frequently referred to as the 'Selby Diversion') between Colton Junction and Templehirst. Part of the abandoned route between Bishopthorpe and Riccall has been converted into a cycle track, though south of Riccall, almost to the site of Barlby North Junction, the erstwhile railway now forms part of the widened and diverted A19 trunk road. The remaining portion of the 1871 line between Selby and Shaftholme Junction continues to be used by Selby-Doncaster local passenger services as far as Templehirst, after which it resumes its original role as the ECML.

Below and right:
Diagrams of York District from WTT's 1948/50. *Author's Collection*

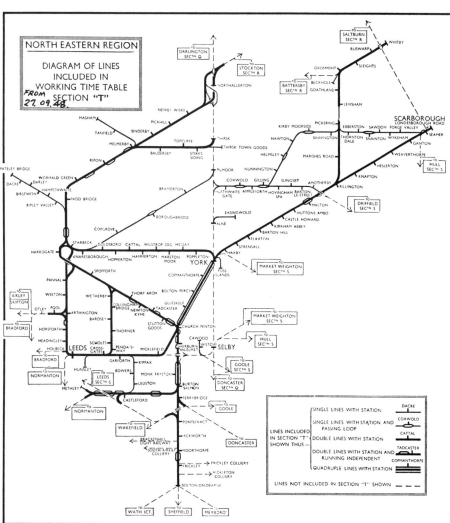

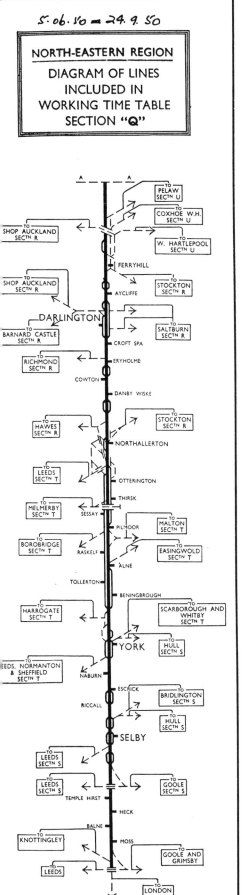

NORTH-EASTERN REGION
DIAGRAM OF LINES
INCLUDED IN
WORKING TIME TABLE
SECTION "Q"

Top:
'B1' No 1202 heads south on the 1871 main line past Bishopthorpe level crossing some three miles out of York with a mixed freight train — possibly in 1947 as 'LNER' appears on the tender. Much of the scene has been incorporated into a new housing development and the main line (closed in 1983) now forms part of the York-Selby cycle route. *Author's Collection*

Above:
An unidentified Class 47 with an up express bound for King's Cross passes over Naburn Bridge on 11 July 1967. The swing bridge cabin above the passing train became a block post on 3 October 1926, after Naburn North and South boxes were closed, but when this photograph was taken Naburn Bridge box itself had been closed on 2 April 1967, when the area was brought under the control of York box. Actually, the swing bridge was fixed in 1956. *BR*

Right:
Much the same scene at Naburn Bridge on 6 August 1992 with the author standing where the ECML once was! *Mrs C. A. Appleby*

Left:
Also on the route of the present-day cycle track, 'A3' Pacific 60045 *Lemberg* passes Escrick station with an up express in 1949 or 1950. Escrick Station box (almost hidden by the smoke) was renamed Escrick North when the wartime boxes and loops at Escrick South and Riccall North were opened on 8 February 1942. The box survived, though rarely open towards the end, until 1963, and 20 years afterwards in 1983 the ECML through Escrick was closed as well. *C. Ord*

Centre left:
NER Raven 'Z1' Atlantic (LNER Class C7) No 2169 with a down express passing Poppleton Junction in early LNER days. Note the NER brass number plate on the cab side. A pity the smoke obscured the signal box. *H. L. Salmon*

Bottom left:
NER Class G 4-4-0 (rebuilt in 1904 from original 2-4-0 of 1888) with a Harrogate train going on to the branch at Poppleton Junction (Skelton from 1938) – probably in early LNER days. This type of locomotive became LNER Class D23 and No 328 was withdrawn in October 1931. *H. L. Salmon*

ECML Widenings and Resignalling: York-Northallerton

By 1898, additional up and down goods lines had been provided between Poppleton Junction and Skelton Bridge, also between Tollerton and Alne, plus an additional down independent from Thirsk North to Thirsk Avenue. In 1899, the Beningbrough (renamed from Shipton in 1898) and Tollerton section acquired additional up and down lines, and an extension of the existing Thirsk widenings took place from Thirsk Avenue northwards to Otterington. Subsequent improvements in the pre-World War 1 era included a down direction 'dive-under' from Longlands Junction (south of Northallerton), opened on 10 February 1901, which enabled freight trains bound for Tees-side to drop down on to the ex-Leeds Northern route at Boroughbridge Road, in order to pass underneath the ECML just beyond the north end of Northallerton station. Two new junctions, at Northallerton South and Cordio, and the provision of an additional link between the ECML and the ex-Leeds Northern, also formed part of this particular scheme and they were brought into use on the same date. Then in 1911/12, an additional down through platform line at Northallerton, was constructed, together with the extension of existing relief sidings to form new up and down independent lines between Castle Hills and Wiske Moor (north of Northallerton).

However, as an alternative to further widenings, an interesting installation of early automatic signalling was intro-

Left:
'A1' Pacific No 2569 *Gladiateur* passing Skelton Bridge box in May 1927. This box was closed on 11 June 1933 in one of the ECML widening stages, and Poppleton Junction box then controlled the connections with the existing Independent Lines, together with the new Slow Lines points located immediately north of the River Ouse bridge. *H. G. W. Household*

duced between Alne and Thirsk Green Lane during the 1903-05 period. Automatic signals were already a feature of certain North American railroads but the London & South Western (LSWR) was the first UK railway to try them, thus the LSWR installed some low pressure electro-pneumatic automatic semaphore signals, of Westinghouse design, in 1902-04. These were situated at selected locations on the Basingstoke-Salisbury main line; they were of the lower quadrant type, and functioned at a compressed air pressure of 15lb psi. When the intervening sections were unoccupied, their normal position was 'off' (ie, clear). However, when the North Eastern decided to embark upon trials with automatic signalling, they opted for a totally different system which was designed and manufactured by the Hall Signal Co of New York. These were electro-gas lower quadrant semaphores of distinctly North American appearance, and unlike their LSWR counterparts the signal arms stood normally in the 'on' position (ie, danger – or caution in the case of distant signal arms) when the sections were unoccupied, so as to preserve, it was said, the principles of block working.

Immediately, one is almost forced to pose the obvious questions – why electro-gas?. And why was such a source of power as compressed carbonic acid gas chosen? Probably the only reasonable answer must be that at the time the installation was decided upon (in 1902), electro-gas provided the only economical way to achieve power operation of the semaphore arms. No suitable electric motors were then available for this purpose, and to run a compressed air main through some 11 miles of open country was not then considered to be a viable proposition. The carbonic acid gas system lent itself readily to what nowadays might be called the 'power pack' technique – thus for the 11 or so miles between Alne and Thirsk each group of signals had its own self-contained power supply. Each signal had two arms, a home and a distant; the distant being

Right:
Not many photographs of the Hall's Automatic Signals have survived, so this example has been published several times previously. In this view at Sessay, looking south, note the distinctly North American appearance of the signal. The box at Sessay ceased to be regularly manned upon full introduction of automatic working in 1906, and thereafter it was only open as required. The signals and box were swept away in the 1933 resignalling; Sessay box was abolished on 2 April 1933 and replaced by a ground frame for the goods yard connection on the down side. *BR*

Below:
In this photograph of Hall's Automatic 16A, the signal has almost gone back to danger after the locomotive of the down express has passed it and occupied the track circuit ahead. This view was taken approaching Pilmoor. Note the old station buildings, which were replaced in 1942 under the wartime widening scheme. *Crown Copyright; NRM, York*

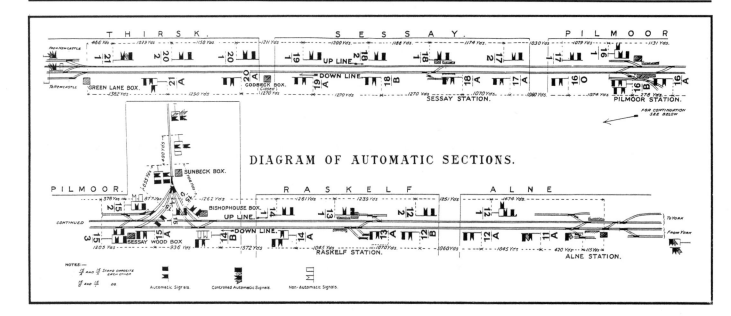

DIAGRAM OF AUTOMATIC SECTIONS.

applicable to the second section ahead. The home signal, providing the section was clear up to and including the overlap of the next signal ahead, assumed the 'off' position when the track circuits two full sections in rear were 'shunted' (ie, occupied by an approaching train), thus bringing the distant signal 'off' one section in front of the train. The motors were operated from cylinders containing carbon-dioxide gas stored at a high pressure, fed through a series of pressure reducing valves. The admission of gas to the motor cylinders, through electrically controlled valves caused the signal arm to move to the 'off' position; return to the 'on' position being by gravity (because the spectacles were heavier than the arms). The control relays and motors were mounted in cases which formed the base of the signal, and the power to drive the arms was transmitted by means of push-rods running up the centre of the tubular steel post. Two gas storage cylinders were provided at each signal post (so one could be removed for filling while the other remained in use), and each full cylinder was said to suffice for around 7,000 operations of the signal arms.

This installation not only doubled the line capacity, but it also permitted some economies to be made – despite what would seem to be the disproportionately high maintenance costs incurred. Fifteen automatic sections were now available in the Alne-Thirsk 'bottle-neck'; Codbeck box was closed (this was a 'break-section' box between Sessay and Green Lane), and the boxes at Sessay and Raskelf were reduced to 'porter-signalman' status, being opened only for local shunting purposes with the 'pickup' (or in exceptional circumstances such as foggy weather). Alne, Sessay Wood and Green Lane were open continuously, and two other boxes at Pilmoor Station and Bishophouse were open only when branch trains were running. The signals were identified by mileage numbers from York, with a letter suffix for down signals and a number suffix for those in the up

direction. Trains were described from box to box by block bell only, though block instruments were retained for use during fog or falling snow when automatic working was (by instruction) suspended.

Work started on this scheme in 1903, and on 31 October 1904 the new signalling was commissioned, though not available for use until inspected by the Board of Trade. Provisional approval was eventually given on 4 June 1905, subject to certain minor modifications being carried out, and automatic working finally began in earnest in February 1906. Incidentally, these signals continued to give good service until they were gradually replaced by colour lights in the 1933 ECML widening and resignalling schemes. (The LSWR automatics actually lasted much longer and the final survivors disappeared around 1966 in the Basingstoke power box scheme.)

The next big event was the 1933 main line widening and resignalling which completely transformed both the appearance and the methods of working of the ECML between Skelton Bridge and Northallerton. A continuous run of colour light signals replaced the traditional semaphores along with the 'Hall's Automatics, and some new station buildings – of quite distinctive appearance – were erected at many locations. (In point of fact, the 1933 resignalling was preceded by two earlier installations north of Northallerton – these being Eryholme-

Right:
Rear view of the 1933 signal box at Beningbrough. Note the prewar LNER style of signal box architecture. Built immediately behind the old structure (which was demolished during the weekend of 27/28 May 1933 to allow the new Up Slow Line to be laid across the site it occupied), the new box was commissioned on 28 May 1933. It was closed on 3 November 1963 though the empty shell remained *in situ* until demolition during 1986. *J. M. Boyes*

Above:
Hall's Automatic Signals (1906).
Author's Collection

Black Banks in 1928, and Cowton-Wiske Moor in 1932.)

During 1933, three separate widenings were completed – between Skelton Bridge-Beningbrough, Alne-Pilmoor (down only) and Otterington-Northallerton – so quadruple track now existed from Poppleton Junction to Alne, and from Thirsk to Northallerton. (Between Alne and Pilmoor, only an additional down line was provided.) At the Northallerton end, a new burrowing line to the south of Northallerton station complemented the 1901 dive-under on the down side, so after 16 July 1933 up freight trains from Tees-side could use the low level route via Boroughbridge Road to gain independent access to the up slow line towards Thirsk. (The new bridge which takes the up Longlands Loop underneath the ECML was constructed in 1931 but it could not be brought into use until resignalling was completed.)

Above:
'A4' No 60007 (formerly No 4498) *Sir Nigel Gresley* passes Tollerton with the down 'Talisman' during the late 1950s. The station buildings, as well as the signal box in the right background, date from the 1899 widening between Alne and Tollerton. The signal box here was replaced by a NE Region-style power box, situated on the up side of the line, which opened on 29 January 1961. The 'new' power box was closed on 10 December 1989 when control of the Tollerton area passed to York IECC. (At the time of writing, the box is still there with the windows boarded up.) *C. Ord*

Centre right:
Alne station looking south on 2 June 1957. 'D20' No 62387 passes through on the Down Slow Line with a railway enthusiasts' special train, The Easingwold bay was behind the group of people standing on the up platform. Alne new box opened on 19 March 1933, and it was closed on 15 May 1960. *J. W. Armstrong*

Right:
The dive-under bridge at the south end of Northallerton station where the Up Longlands Loop line burrows beneath the ECML to enable freight trains from Tees-side to gain access to the Up Slow Line towards Thirsk, thus avoiding conflict at High Junction with up ECML traffic. Construction started in October 1930 and bridgework was completed in June 1931. However, the facility could not be brought into use until 16 July 1933 pending construction of the widening to Otterington, together with the completion of resignalling. The signal box on the main line to the right of the picture was Northallerton South, a wooden structure opened in 1898 and closed on 16 July 1933. *BR*

Right:
Raskelf station looking north during the 1950s. The down platform became an island between the existing Down Main and the new Down Slow line in the 1933 widening. The up side buildings were demolished in 1959, the station having been closed to passengers from 5 May 1958, so that the new Up Slow line between Pilmoor and Alne could be laid. The box here was closed on 7 September 1958. *J. W. Armstrong*

Four intermediate stations were affected by the widenings; Alne was rebuilt on the down side only, though complete rebuilding (in a rather striking prewar LNER style of architecture) was necessary at Beningbrough and Otterington. Raskelf retained its up platform, though a new booking office was built outside at road level, but the down platform had to be rebuilt as an island to accommodate the new Down Slow line.

However, Tollerton station did not need to be altered, having been completely rebuilt in a previous widening which took place during 1898/99. The resignalling involved the building of new boxes to replace old structures at Ben-

Above:
Engineering operations in progress at Thirsk on 3 June 1932. By this time preparations were actively in hand for the major resignalling scheme which came to fruition during November 1933. This particular work involved the laying in of a complete scissors crossing. Note the high-visibility vest had not yet been invented! The signal box in this photograph, Thirsk Middle, was built in 1895 and it was one of five manual boxes to be displaced by the Thirsk new power box erected in 1933 on a site just off picture to the right of the three men bending down. *BR*

Right:
Exterior of Thirsk box taken in 1936. This very modern looking box was opened in two stages; on 5 November 1933 it displaced Avenue and Thirsk North boxes, then on 19 November 1933, Thirsk Middle, Thirsk South and Green Lane boxes were closed. Thirsk box was closed under the York IECC scheme at 22.10 on Saturday 20 January 1990, though the redundant structure was not demolished until Sunday 17 March 1991. *BR*

Far right:
Interior view of Thirsk box showing the route setting panel as originally installed in 1933. *BR*

ingbrough, Alne, Sessay Wood, Thirsk and Otterington. At certain other boxes such as Tollerton, Raskelf and Pilmoor, modernisation of the interior equipment was achieved within the existing structures. Also, at both extremities of the scheme, the boxes of that time at Poppleton Junction (called Skelton from 1938), and Northallerton High Junction were suitably adapted for the new signalling. A number of intermediate boxes were closed under this scheme, such as Skel-

ton Bridge, Hunting Bridge, Newton Siding, Bishophouse, Sessay, Huttons Wood and Northallerton South. The latter named box had previously overtaken the functions of Longlands and Cordio boxes as long ago as 1926. A level crossing at Overton, south of Beningbrough, was also superseded from 24 October 1932 by an overbridge as a result of the widenings.

The colour light signals were of the 'searchlight' type popular with signal

Below:
Looking northwards at Thirsk on 3 June 1932 from the same site shown in the previous photograph. Note the vast amount of infrastructure compared with the present day. Thirsk Up Yard is to the right of the main lines, and Down Yard to the left. The signal box in the distance was Thirsk North. *BR*

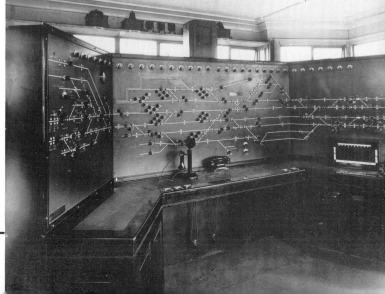

engineers during the 1930s, and purely automatic signals were approach lighted. Three aspect signalling was usual, though in closely signalled areas (such as Thirsk) a fourth 'double yellow' aspect was introduced. Most unfortunately, when the Gresley high-speed era commenced in 1935, a 'speed ceiling' had to be imposed upon the York-Darlington stretch of ECML because of insufficient braking distances for high-speed running. (A start was made upon conversion to four aspect signalling after the 'Coronation' was introduced in 1937, but the outbreak of World War 2 in 1939 postponed completion of this work.)

The most significant resignalling of this period occurred at Thirsk, where a completely new concept of route setting switches geographically located on the control panel was installed in an impressive looking modern box. The area covered by the new route relay interlocking at Thirsk extended over something like four miles – extremely small by present day standards, but probably one of the largest areas to be controlled by one box back in the 1930s, and certainly a 'first' for a route setting switch panel. Five manual boxes were closed after Thirsk box was opened in two stages on 5 and 19 November 1933 (ie, Green Lane, Thirsk South, Thirsk Middle, Thirsk North and Avenue), and without doubt, Thirsk was not only a landmark in signalling history but it was also the forerunner of modern signalling practice as we now know it. The improvements of the 1930s were inspected during February and April 1934 by the Minister of Transport's Inspecting Officer, Lt-Col E. Woodhouse, who concluded that 'The works carried out in connection with this extensive scheme, the signalling side of which embodies many interesting and novel features, appeared to be of first class construction and in good order', and subject to a few minor observations being given attention, he recommended that ministerial approval be given.

By the summer of 1939, another major resignalling scheme was well advanced, affecting Northallerton and the ECML northwards up to and including the Darlington station area. A large new power box was built at Northallerton, which contained a Westinghouse One Control Switch (OCS) panel, and it was commissioned on that most auspicious of dates – Sunday 3 September 1939! Northallerton new box overtook the functions of the former High Junction box (situated directly opposite to it), plus Castle Hills and Wiske Moor on the main line to the north, and Northallerton West just round the corner on the Hawes branch.

Heavy wartime traffic brought further widenings and some more resignalling during 1942, in an attempt to ease the congestion caused by there being only two tracks through Thirsk station, and between Green Lane and Pilmoor. New up and down slow lines were constructed at Thirsk station, together with platform

Above:

Northallerton Signal Boxes. *R. D. Pulleyn*

faces, and additional running lines were provided southwards to Pilmoor. It was also necessary to rebuild both Sessay and Pilmoor stations.

To keep the amount of new signalling work down to a minimum, bearing in mind wartime shortages of men, materials and equipment, these additional lines between Thirsk and Pilmoor were designated as goods lines and permissive working applied for freight trains. As always, a complication arose because the intermediate station at Sessay still required to be served by a few stopping passenger trains, so in 1942 a new signal box had to be provided (at Sessay) and a method of Absolute Block working devised to cater for the early morning and evening passenger service. (This arrangement, using 'Block Conversion'

tickets persisted until 1958 when Sessay station was closed.) The wartime goods lines were upgraded and resignalled to become slow lines in 1959, as a prelude to the up side widening between Pilmoor and Alne which at long last was achieved in 1960.

Resignalling at Pilmoor took place on 15 May 1960, and the new up slow line was opened to traffic on 19 June 1960, thus marking the completion of quadruple track all the way, in both directions, between Skelton Bridge and Northallerton. At Pilmoor, the former Pilmoor Station box had been named Pilmoor North from 19 February 1943; similarly, Sessay

Right:

Signalman Ted Welch at work on the Northallerton OCS panel shortly after the installation was commissioned on Sunday 3 September 1939. The remote junctions at Longlands (top) and Cordio (bottom) can be seen at the right hand end of the panel, and the Northallerton Loop to and from Northallerton East towards the top left. The Hawes branch is at the bottom left, though the low level lines shown in outline only at the bottom were at that time controlled by Boroughbridge Road box. At the extreme left hand end, the Castle Hills-Wiske Moor loops can just be made out. This impressive diagram was replaced in 1974, after a lot of rationalisation had been carried out, but the switch console (shortened somewhat) remained in use until the box was closed under the York IECC scheme on 15 April 1990. *BR*

Right:

Northallerton box looking north from the down platform on 22 April 1984. The line to the right is the route now traversed by the TransPennine Liverpool-Middlesbrough services introduced on 14 May 1992. *L. Abram*

Below:

A grubby-looking 'V2' No 918 (formerly No 4889) heads a down train composed of mixed coaching stock past Northallerton box in August 1947. *BR*

Left:
Thirsk station looking south on 15 May 1943. The two platforms had recently been converted into islands, the outer faces being for the newly constructed slow lines. *BR*

Centre left:
Christmas Eve, 24 December 1941 and a down freight train hauled by 'Q6' 0-8-0 No 1284 passes through the soon-to-be demolished overbridge at the south end of Sessay station. It is interesting to note that military personnel were involved in demolition of the bridge by explosives, which was a necessary pre-requisite of widening to four tracks which took place during 1942. *BR*

Bottom left:
The 1942 widening scheme involved the provision of a new signal box at Sessay. This photograph taken on 20 March 1959, is a good example of a LNER (NE area) wartime signal box. The box became fully operational on 9 August 1942, but it was only open as required to deal with the infrequent passenger services which called at Sessay. After the closure of Sessay station to passengers from 15 September 1958 the box was 'switched out', and it was abolished upon resignalling of the wartime goods lines to slow lines status in 1959. *BR*

Below:
A much later view of Sessay station on 4 June 1977 looking northwards. Sulzer Class 46 No 46011, at speed with an up express, passes the remains of what had been a completely rebuilt station in 1942. The site has since been cleared. *Brian Morrison*

Centre right:
Class 37 No 37219, running on the Down Slow line, passes Pilmoor box on 8 May 1976. The 1960 route setting panel was replaced by an Individual Function Switch (IFS) panel during the weekend of 26/28 June 1971 and the box finally closed on 28 July 1985. The redundant box structure still existed in September 1992. *J. E. Oxley*

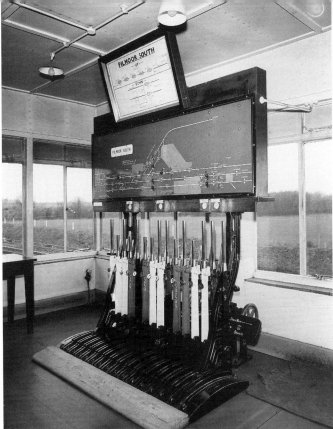

Above left:
Sessay Wood Junction looking south prior to the 1933 widening and resignalling. The branch curving away to the left was the 'North Curve' to Sunbeck – thence on to Gilling where the lines to Malton and Pickering (via Helmsley) diverged. In the far distance was Bishophouse Junction where the 'Raskelf Curve' to Sunbeck formed a triangle. Note the Hall's Automatic signals. When the new Down Slow line was added in 1933, it ran across the site of the old box – thus the replacement (built immediately behind it) was commissioned on 12 March 1933 concurrently with closure and demolition of the old structure.
J. M. Boyes

Above:
Sessay Wood box was renamed Pilmoor South on 19 February 1943, and by the time this photograph was taken on 20 March 1959, the 'Raskelf Curve' between Bishophouse and Sunbeck had been abandoned during the previous month. (Note the taped-over portions on the box diagram.) The panel and frame, commissioned on 12 March 1933 when the box opened, was replaced by a small route setting switch panel on 15 May 1960 upon the closure of Pilmoor North box. Once again this box was renamed, and it became 'Pilmoor'. *BR*

Left:
Pilmoor station looking south on 15 April 1943 after completion of the 1942 widening on the down side. The line to the right was the branch to Boroughbridge and Knaresborough, which lost its passenger service after the last trains ran on Saturday 23 September 1950. Thereafter, the line between Pilmoor and Brafferton was closed completely, but the remainder of the branch lingered on for freight traffic until 2 October 1964. *BR*

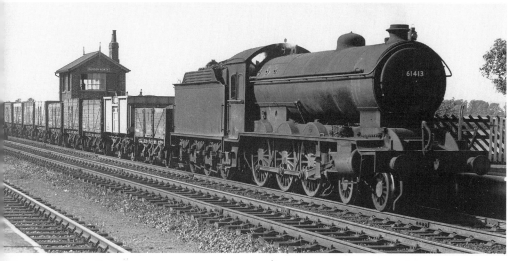

Left:
Class B16/1 No 61413 passing Pilmoor North box with a mid-1950s up freight train. The 1942 widening on the up side terminated at Pilmoor North, and the 1960 continuation thereof through to Alne (opened 19 June 1960) ran over the site of this box and the up platform.
G. W. Sharpe

Below left:
World War 2 widening activity in progress looking north at Skelton Bridge, showing construction of the new Down Slow line bridge over the River Ouse parallel with the existing GNE bridge of 1841, which continues to carry present day ECML traffic. This wartime bridge was opened on 18 October 1942, and it is still in use. *BR*

effect that despite wartime difficulties, the works reflected credit on all concerned and except in a few minor details, they did not fall short of the company's usual high standard. He had no hesitation in recommending Ministerial approval being given.

For the record, numerous other alterations took place during the 1960s. At Thirsk, following removal of the junction with the Melmerby branch (which had closed from 14 September 1959), considerable rationalisation of the track layout eventually resulted in replacement of the vintage 1933-style route setting panel by a smaller, much simplified 'NX' version on 19 September 1965. Then during the early 1970s the fast line platform faces at Thirsk were removed, in preparation for high speed running, thus leaving the station to be served by the wartime slow line platforms only. At Northallerton considerable simplification of the layout also occurred, especially following closure of the Leeds Northern route from Harrogate via Ripon in 1967, and the large imposing 1939 panel was subsequently replaced, though the OCS console remained in use (suitably modified) until the box itself was closed under the York IECC scheme in 1990.

Also, the 1960 widening at Alne swept away the last traces of the Alne & Easingwold Light Railway (opened on 25 July 1891) which had previously used a short bay platform on the up side. The 'Easingwold' passenger service had been withdrawn from 29 November 1948, though the company struggled on with gradually diminishing freight traffic until its eventual demise on 27 December 1957.

The 'Selby Diversion'

The first railway to reach Selby was the Leeds & Selby which opened on 22 September 1834, and terminated in what is now the goods depot alongside the present passenger station. The second line was the Hull & Selby which opened on 1 July 1840, and crossed the River Ouse by means of a bascule type lifting bridge.

Wood became Pilmoor South from the same date. On 15 May 1960, Pilmoor North was closed, and the South box (where a new panel was provided in place of the 1933 hybrid frame and panel installation) became 'Pilmoor'. At the same time, the box at Alne was closed, and on 29 January 1961 a new box at Tollerton was opened. (More recently, Pilmoor box was closed on 28 July 1985.)

The other major piece of wartime work was carried out at Skelton Bridge where a new bridge was constructed to carry an additional down line over the River Ouse. This bridge was brought into use on 18 October 1942, after a short portion of new line had been laid to connect the down independent south of the bridge with the down slow immediately to the north thereof. Sufficient space was left available at this site for construction of an additional up line bridge, but, in the event, even though the LNER mentioned such a possibility in their postwar development plan *Forward* (which was published in 1946), it never happened. There was also talk of a fly-over, or a dive-

under, to carry the up slow line across the fast lines somewhere south of Beningbrough in anticipation of such a new bridge being built, but desirable as this facility might have been, it was extremely difficult to justify, hence the idea never even got off the drawing board.

The provision of Skelton New Sidings in 1942 was preceded by the opening of a large electro-mechanical box at Skelton on 8 June 1941. This wartime box contained a frame of 75 levers, and some thumb-switches located on a panel to control the remote connections at Skelton Bridge. Eventually, after the closure of Skelton New Sidings early in 1977, the junction at Skelton was extensively remodelled, and a new entrance-exit (NX) panel to replace the wartime electro-mechanical installation, was commissioned on 13 March 1977.

The aforementioned wartime works between Thirsk and Skelton were inspected on 19 August 1943 by Major G. R. S. Wilson on behalf of the Minister of War Transport, and in the conclusion to his report he praised the LNER to the

Above:
A unique view of Thirsk box interior taken on 20 April 1965. Note the new 'NX' panel in situ which replaced the 1933 panel on 19 September 1965. *BR*

Above right:
A close up shot of Thirsk new 'NX' panel on 20 April 1965. Note the considerable degree of track simplification depicted on this panel which was commissioned on 19 September 1965. *BR*

Right:
Thirsk station looking northwards on 28 March 1978, with Class 37 No 37003 passing through on the Up Fast line with a southbound freight train. Note the fast line platform faces have by now been removed. *C. R. Davis*

Below:
Thirsk station on 28 September 1988 after complete rebuilding in modern style. Electrification masts had recently been erected. *BR*

Above:
An old picture of the original Selby bascule-type lifting bridge in the closed to river position. *BR*

Above right:
The same bridge at Selby in the closed to rail position. From 1871, this antiquated bridge carried ECML traffic for 20 years until it was replaced by the present swing bridge situated in the foreground to this vintage photograph. *BR*

Right:
'A3' Pacific No 60039 *Sandwich* **heads an up express freight through Selby on 13 December 1962. The 1891 swing bridge cabin can be seen in the background, with Selby North box to the left. Selby North was the first of the Selby boxes to be closed (on 18 April 1971) under the Selby resignalling scheme, though the derelict structure managed to survive for many years.** *J. S. Whiteley*

The two companies then established a through station which enabled services between Leeds and Hull to operate. The ECML, which opened on 2 January 1871, utilised the old route through Selby, though the NER built a much larger station (the present one) in 1898/99. The antiquated bascule lifting bridge was replaced by a hydraulically operated swing bridge, located slightly down-river from the original, in 1891. The swing bridge tended to be the 'Achilles' Heel' of the ECML, and the speed restrictions in the locality were always detrimental to high speed running.

During development of the Selby Coalfield project in the 1970s, it was accepted by the then National Coal Board (now British Coal) that if coal was to be extracted from beneath the existing ECML north of Selby, then speed restrictions would become inevitable – which would completely negate BR's aspirations to introduce high speed train services. In any event, BR was only too well aware that the unusual geology of its ECML in this area would cause difficulty in maintaining a stable and sound formation for high speed running, and it was duly agreed between the two parties that rather than leave a pillar of support under the line – and thus sterilise over 40 million tonnes of coal – it would be preferable to divert the the ECML away from the proposed coalfield altogether, and thereafter the planning proceeded on this basis.

A parliamentary submission for construction of a new high speed route avoiding the proposed coalfield was made during 1977, and the BR (Selby) Act 1978 received the Royal Assent on

26 July 1979. The new line, designed for 125 mph running throughout, is some 14½ miles in length, and it extends from Templehirst (south of Selby) to a junction with the (ex Y&NM) York-Church Fenton line at Colton. The Leeds-Selby line, diverted slightly northwards from its original formation in the vicinity of Hambleton, now crosses over the top of the new main line, and a single line connection – the Hambleton North East curve – joins the Selby line to form a through route between York and Selby/Hull. Similarly, a double line connection – called the Hambleton South

Above:
An InterCity 125 set headed by power car No 43100 coming off Selby swing bridge on 7 April 1983, with the derelict Selby North box still in evidence 12 years after closure! *M. J. Collins*

Above right:
Colton Junction on 29 September 1983, the day on which the ECML 'Selby Diversion' was opened throughout. This was the first purpose-built high speed junction on BR specially designed for 125mph running. The new main line towards Templehirst can be seen curving away to the left and the quadruple track to Church Fenton continues through the bridge to the centre of the picture. *BR*

Right:
June 1983 and a Hull-York DMU crosses the new River Wharfe viaduct, situated on the Hambleton-Colton section of the 'Selby Diversion' – the northern part of which was opened on 16 May 1983. *BR*

West curve – joins the Leeds line to form a through route for such as the Immingham-Leeds (Hunslet) oil trains.

Concurrently with development of the new main line project, the closure procedure was invoked in order to abandon the existing (1871) line between Barlby North and Chaloners Whin. Control of the new railway was centred upon York box, which acquired an additional panel. The new panel was a Westinghouse M5 'NX' type, and it was designed to control the territory between the former Chaloners Whin Junction and just south of Templehirst to interface with Doncaster power box. It also controlled the lines to Church Fenton (exclusive), together with the new junctions at Hambleton, and intervened on a short portion of the Leeds-Selby line between Selby and Gascoigne Wood.

The northern end of the new line was opened first. Under the resignalling, the boxes at Copmanthorpe and Bolton Percy were closed on 12/13 March 1983, and the Church Fenton end of the new panel at York was then made operative. Shortly afterwards, the new ECML junction at Colton was commissioned, and from 9/10 April 1983 the new panel then interfaced additionally with Selby and Gascoigne Wood boxes. During the summer of 1983, the northern end of the new line was used by the York-Selby/Hull services and by the end of

September what became known as 'Operation Big Switch' was ready for introduction. This involved a complete diversion of all ECML services via Knottingley and Askern for a full week (the pre-1871 route in effect) to enable the new junction at Templehirst to be laid in, together with the completion of extensive signalling work.

After 23.30 on Saturday 24 September 1983, the old main line between Chaloners Whin and Barlby North was taken out of use and the Knottingley diversion commenced. By the following Sunday night, 2 October 1983, the new main line was opened for traffic throughout and the full service was resumed as planned on Monday morning 3 October. The new panel at York now interfaced with Doncaster; it also worked with Selby from Templehirst along that part of the old main line still retained for local services, as well as on the Selby-Leeds line east of Hambleton. Included in the resignalling was a new set of connections south of Dringhouses, which assumed the name 'Dringhouses Junction' in order to give access to and from the Leeds lines and Dringhouses Yard. (In the event, these new connections were to be short-lived as Dringhouses Yard only lasted for a few years thereafter.)

Initially, train speeds over the new main line were restricted to allow the track to bed down, though the restric-

tions were progressively eased. Full 125 mph running was not scheduled until commencement of the May 1984 timetable.

Finally, it is of interest to note that the 1951 Outer South panel in York box had previously extended its sphere of influence southwards in two stages during 1967. Firstly, the boxes at Naburn and Escrick South were closed from 2 April 1967, then York worked with Riccall North. In the second stage, which involved the provision of three Automatic Half Barrier (AHB) level crossings at York Road, Riccall South and Turnhead, the boxes at Riccall North and South were closed and York worked to Barlby North from 11 June 1967. (The AHB crossings were monitored by Barlby North rather than York.) The subsequent story of Selby resignalling, which developed piecemeal during the 1970s, is really beyond the scope of this particular book: suffice it to say that the present 'NX' panel at Selby (former West) box, which no longer has any ECML involvement, was originally installed in Selby South box (in 1972) and physically transferred to its present location during 1973.

Pre-Electrification Alterations at York

Before attempting to describe the extensive alterations to the York station track layout that took place during 1988/89 as a necessary pre-requisite to both the 1989 resignalling and the electrification which followed, it is, perhaps, appropriate to recall an earlier rationalisation of the north end which occurred in 1974. Between 17 and 29 April 1974, a large scale simplification was undertaken which involved the removal of Waterworks Crossing, remodelling the northern end of the then Platform 14, and repositioning certain connections to conform with the resultant layout. This was a major job, involving disconnections and handsignalling for a fortnight, and upon completion of the work, access between the former Platforms 14/15/16 and the Scarborough branch was no longer possible – something which applies to this very day. Furthermore, the direct link between York Yard South and the Scarborough direction was severed.

Subsequently, track layout alterations and resignalling work took place early in 1983 in connection with the then new Clifton carriage maintenance and servicing facilities, and a purpose-built control tower, equipped with an individual function switch (IFS) type of panel was commissioned on 6 February 1983. (This panel was predominantly concerned with internal depot shunting operations, but when the adjacent running lines became involved for movements to and from the sidings, it was subject to release by York box.)

Work started during 1988 on what was then undoubtedly the largest and most complex track and signalling project undertaken by BR since the remodelling at Crewe in 1985. The objective was to slim down the mass of junctions, points and crossings that formed the approaches to both ends of York station into a

faster and more economical layout. At the same time, preparations were taking place, for both the installation of a highly sophisticated solid state interlocking system (SSI) and the forthcoming electrification of the ECML. However, unlike the Crewe remodelling, BR's engineers and contractors did not have the benefit of a total blockade while they physically

Below:
A much simplified York north end layout on 22 April 1980, looking over the site of Waterworks Crossing (removed 1974) towards Scarborough Bridge. *BR*

Bottom:
The complicated layout at Clifton, also very much in need of rationalisation, taken on 22 April 1980 prior to 'like for like' renewal in 1981. *BR*

Above left:
A close up shot of the Chaloners Whin layout in the upper portion of York Box Outer South panel on 26 August 1969. Note the out of scale insert which covered the additional territory absorbed after the closure of Naburn and Escrick South boxes on 2 April 1967, followed by a subsequent stage when Riccall North and South boxes closed on 11 June 1967. The three AHB level crossings at Riccall, although shown on the York Box diagram, were supervised by the then fringe box at Barlby North (Selby). *BR*

Left:
A rather unusual shot of the Selby 'NX' panel when it was installed at Selby South box in 1972. Subsequently, the panel was transferred to Selby West box (now called 'Selby') in 1973, but since 1983 it has been considerably altered and, of course, it no longer controls the ECML. *BR*

Left:
An unusual view of the complex at York south end taken from the station roof on 22 April 1980. *BR*

Below:
A civil engineering nightmare! Another York south end view (on 22 April 1980) to compare with some of the present-day photographs which appear later herein. *BR*

Right:
Overnight engineering work in progress on 19 January 1989 at Platform 5 (9) during the erection of overhead line equipment. *BR*

Below right:
York south end during extensive track layout alterations. Note the then newly erected IECC building to left centre of picture. *BR*

completed the final stages of the job, so the York scheme had to be carried out in three main stages, each being divided into specific work sites. Self sufficiency was of paramount importance in the success or otherwise of this venture, thus vital materials were stockpiled at strategically located sites, so that everything was readily to hand once the pre-planned possessions were taken for work to commence. The two main stockpile sites, where track could be pre-assembled, were at Dringhouses and Clifton – both of which had been closed for traffic purposes during 1987 – with subsidiary sites established near to the west side of the station and at York Yard South. Provision also had to be made for the storage of stone ballast, and the dumping of spoil and scrap material recovered from old track after removal.

During Stages 1 and 2, between 10 September and 28 November 1988, the north end approaches were further simplified, followed by a physical raising of the station footbridge which was carried out over two weekends in December 1988, in order to allow sufficient clearance for the erection of overhead line equipment.

Once successfully completed, attention was moved to the more difficult south end, where work began in earnest starting with Stage 1 on 19 February 1989. Completion of Stage 5 by the target date of 4 June 1989 was achieved as scheduled, and during all the various stages the meticulously planned arrangements to deal with trains in what was virtually half a station at any one time worked out remarkably well in practice. Also, during this period, Hol-

gate Road bridge was lifted by means of hydraulic jacks placed at each of the four corners, so as to give adequate clearance for the electrification wires.

Prior to commissioning of the new signal box, (or Integrated Electronic Control Centre [IECC] to give it its proper name), which took place between 11 and 14 May 1989, the up and down avoiding lines between Holgate Junction and Skelton were upgraded in status from 'goods' lines to 'slow' lines with effect from 21 August 1988 and thereafter worked under Track Circuit Block (TCB) regulations so as to be readily available for use by passenger trains as and when necessary. Also, upon comple-

tion of signalling work at York Yard North over the same weekend, the last few remaining semaphore signals there were replaced by colour lights.

Several other alterations took place around this same period, so that the final track layout became compatible with both the new signalling and the electrification which was soon to follow.

One notable example of the ongoing rationalisation was the removal of the main lines through the centre of the station, which were taken out of use from 8 November 1988; also, during the north end alterations the then Platform 12 and all but one of the bay platforms in the 'Scarborough Corner' lost their tracks.

Above:
Rationalisation of York south end in progress. The extent of simplification achieved has to be seen to be believed!
BR

The degree of simplification achieved is made all the more noteworthy by the fact that only one diamond crossing now remains in the whole of the York station layout, this being where the line between Platform 5 (9) and the Scarborough branch crosses the up main line from the north leading towards Platform 3 (8) – a far cry from the erstwhile Waterworks Crossing. Needless to say that in this day and age it is absolutely imperative that track layouts are simplified to the maximum possible extent, consistent with business and operational requirements, in order to contain the cost of modernisation projects within reasonable limits: and this is exactly what happened at York.

York Integrated Electronic Control Centre (IECC) – Stage Work

The new signalling was commissioned on Sunday 14 May 1989, and the station platforms were renumbered at the same time. At precisely 00.01 on Thursday 11 May 1989, the four Westinghouse OCS panels in the 1951 York box were taken out of use, and the boxes at York Yard South, York Yard North and Skelton were closed. On the Scarborough branch, the boxes at Burton Lane and Bootham had previously closed on 30 April 1989, thus the 'old' York box was already working with the fringe box at Strensall. During the intervening period between 11 and 14 May 1989, traffic was worked through the York IECC area under 'Emergency Block' arrangements supplemented by handsignalmen, equipped with radios, stationed at various strategic locations.

The IECC actually took over at 07.08 on Sunday 14 May 1989 and the territory it initially controlled interfaced with Tollerton (ECML north), Poppleton (Harrogate branch), Strensall (Scarborough branch) and, as a temporary measure, the 1983 'Selby Diversion' NX panel in the 'old' York box. Subsequently, this one remaining panel in the old box was dispensed with at 00.33 on Sunday 10 September 1989, so the IECC then interfaced southwards with Doncaster power box (ECML south), Church Fenton (Leeds and Normanton lines), Gascoigne Wood and Selby (Leeds-Hull line) and again with Selby on the remaining portion of the 1871 main line which effectively is now a branch from Templehirst Junction.

Going northwards, Tollerton box was closed on 10 December 1989, closely followed by Thirsk which surrendered its territory to the IECC at 22.10 on Saturday 20 January 1990. This then only left

Right:
A classic overview of night time engineering work at the south end of York station in March 1989. The floodlighting of York Minster provides an ancient backdrop to this modern scene. *BR*

Bottom right:
Looking through Holgate Bridge towards York station in 1989 at the time that the bridge was being raised to permit the erection of overhead line equipment. *BR*

Northallerton to be dealt with, and upon completion of another resignalling exercise, which was conducted over the Easter weekend of 1990, control of the Northallerton box area was passed to the IECC at 01.30 on Sunday 15 April 1990. This tall brick structure, situated on the up side of the line just north of Northallerton station and quite a local landmark, was demolished shortly afterwards to permit energisation of the overhead line equipment.

At this stage, York IECC fringed with Darlington (former South) power box on the ECML and with Low Gates on the (ex-Leeds Northern) line towards Teesside. Finally, after Darlington box was closed under the last stages of Newcastle resignalling, York and Tyneside IECC's interfaced with each other in the Wiske Moor-Danby Wiske locality, a couple of miles or so north of Northallerton, during the weekend of 11/12 May 1991.

On the ex-Leeds Northern route towards Tees-side, from a short distance north of Long Lane level crossing – which at present is the next block post beyond Low Gates – it was originally planned that York IECC would link up with Bowesfield box (which actually is located on the Darlington-Saltburn line near Thornaby, but it controls the junction at Eaglescliffe). York IECC now exercises control over the low level route at Northallerton, together with the junction at Northallerton East (previously worked by Low Gates from 6 March 1960), though the two intermediate CCTV level crossings at Boroughbridge Road and Romanby are still controlled by Low Gates, who also monitors the AHB crossing at Springwell Lane, even though these crossings come within the protection of York IECC signals. (The York [Y] signals in question are, of course, 'slotted' by Low Gates.)

In the final analysis it was planned that Low Gates would become a control point for the various level crossings in the locality – in effect a glorified gate box. However, all the signs are that this particular part of the scheme might well be reappraised, so in the meantime, Low Gates will continue to perform its 'hybrid' function both as a fringe box to the IECC and as a block post towards Long Lane. (Additionally, Low Gates continues to monitor the AHB crossing at Brompton where the box was closed as long ago as 9 October 1966.)

Above:
York IECC on 18 May 1989, a week after the initial commissioning. Supervisor Ernie Elvidge (recently retired from BR) maintains a close watch upon the current situation by means of the overview VDUs positioned on his desk (the 'Supervisor's Workstation'). Only the three screens on the left were in use when this photograph was taken; the two screens on the right were inoperative because at that time Tollerton, Thirsk and Northallerton boxes were still open. The signalman in the background is operating the 'North Workstation'. *BR*

Left:
Another York IECC interior view, also taken on 18 May 1989. The 'South Workstation' is on the left and the 'North Workstation' to the right. The working environment is totally different from that in a conventional power box. *BR*

Below left:
In this photograph, taken on 18 May 1989 from behind the 'Supervisor's Workstation', the overview screens of the Hambleton/Colton area and both ends of York itself are clearly visible. *BR*

Right:
York IECC — Present track layouts in the controlled area. *R. D. Pulleyn*

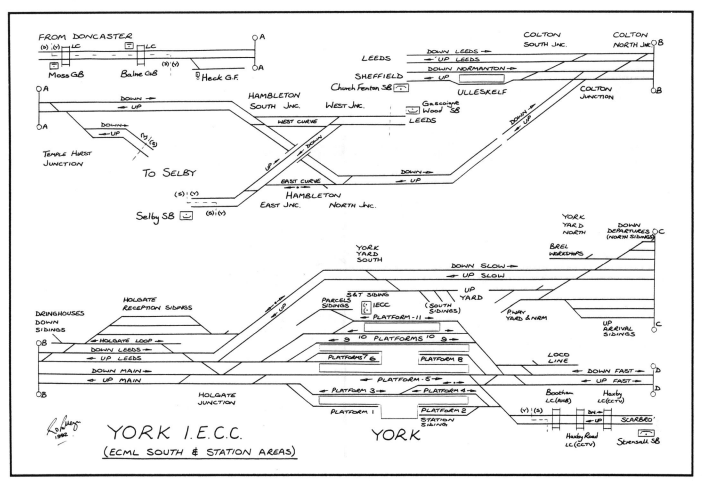

YORK I.E.C.C.
(ECML SOUTH & STATION AREAS)

YORK

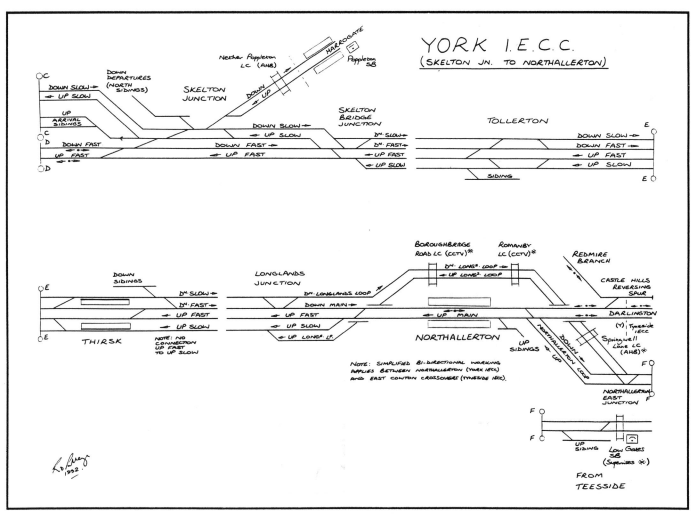

YORK I.E.C.C.
(SKELTON JN. TO NORTHALLERTON)

Left:
The 06.00 King's Cross-Aberdeen HST approaches Northallerton on Saturday 14 April 1990. (The train is passing over the bridge through which the Up Longlands Loop passes underneath the ECML.) By this time 'Emergency Block Working' was in force under the supervision of York IECC. Note signal Y474 had replaced former signal N111 just behind it, and full control of the Northallerton box area was passed to York IECC at 01.30 on Sunday 15 April 1990. *I. S. Carr*

York IECC and the Redmire Branch

Although strictly speaking not part of the ECML infrastructure saga, it is of interest to note the unusual involvement that York IECC had in signalling movements on and off the Redmire branch via the reversing spur at Castle Hills following the closure of Northallerton box from 15 April 1990. Actually, the single line train staff for the 'One Train Working' (OTW) section to Bedale, along with the keys for the various train crew operated (TMO) level crossings en route, was kept at Low Gates when not in use because the daily freight train ran to and from Tees-side. Latterly, the Redmire branch was all that remained of the former Wensleydale line to Hawes (and Garsdale) which lost its passenger service from Northallerton back in 1954, and which was closed completely west of Redmire 10 years later. Normally the line was traversed by just one daily freight service in each direction – ie, 6N53 (Redcar-Redmire) which returned as 6N54 (Redmire-Tees Yard) – and it was, in effect, a siding some 22 miles long operated on a minimum-cost basis. Recently, only one intermediate staffed level crossing remained – which was at Bedale, where both road and rail conditions were patently unsuitable to allow for the withdrawal of attendance. Bedale box, downgraded to gate box status on 5 February 1985, was reinstated as a block post on 8 April 1990. This was done not so much for traffic purposes, but rather to facilitate weekday engineering possessions between Northallerton and Bedale, while the daily freight train occupied the Bedale-Redmire (OTW) section.

The staple traffic flow was crushed limestone from Redmire Quarry to British Steel's works at Redcar. However, a serious problem arose early in 1992 when British Steel announced their intention to cease using rail transport in favour of road haulage, and it looked very much as if the line would close after the existing contract ran out on 31 March 1992. This led to strong protests in the dale, and, following representations made by the local MP, a temporary reprieve was granted for six months in order to allow top-level discussions to be held involving British Steel, Trainload Freight and the North Yorkshire County Council – the latter body being particularly concerned about the proposed switch from rail to road in an environmentally-sensitive area of beautiful countryside.

Subsequently, British Steel indicated that the needs of its Redcar works could henceforth continue to be met by rail from one of their own quarries at Hardendale, near Shap, (which once supplied the now-closed Ravenscraig steel works) rather than from Wensleydale, which effectively sealed the fate of the Redmire branch. The last freight train ran on Friday 18 December 1992 hauled by Thornaby-based locomotive No 60086.

The final trains over the Redmire branch proved to be three charter specials, which ran on Monday 28 December 1992 (from Swindon), Tuesday 29 December 1992 (from Crewe) and Saturday 2 January 1993 (from King's Cross). In each case the charter specials were 'topped and tailed' by Thornaby-based Class 37s. The branch only just survived into 1993, and it is now officially regarded as closed to traffic.

York IECC Described

Located in a purpose-built structure on the site of the former 'Fruit Dock' area immediately to the west of Platforms 10/11 (15/16), the IECC is an entirely new concept which represents the ultimate in state-of-the-art signalling technology based upon Solid State Interlocking (SSI) and the use of computerised aids.

Instead of the conventional type of NX route setting panels which are to be found in the majority of modern installations, the signalmen at York now exercise control and oversight by means of visual display units (VDUs), and in normal circumstances trains can be routed automatically by an 'Automatic Route Setting' system (ARS) interfaced with BR's national computerised timetable data-base that 'recognises' trains by their unique working timetable (WTT) reporting number. While ARS is fine when everything works according to plan – and a range of deviations can be built into the programme – it is necessary to make provision for out of course running, short notice specials, cancellations and, of course, emergency situations. To cater for such eventualities, facilities are provided to enable the signalmen to intervene and take over manual control from ARS on any part of their territory, in which case they then have to set up routes themselves.

There are two signalmen's 'workstations' (ie, North and South), each of which contains a Signalman's Display System (SDS) comprising a bank of VDUs (television screens) capable of giving a selection of 'overview' and 'detail view' displays relative to the area of control. Instead of push buttons or switches, routes can be set up by means of a 'tracker-ball' and cursor, supplemented by a computer-type keyboard, and the whole working environment is completely different from that to be found in a conventional power box. In addition to the two signalmen's workstations, separate displays are provided for the Station Announcer and the box Supervisor (the modern counterpart of the former Traffic Regulator) together with an ancillary position.

The technicians are located in a separate part of the building, and they are assisted by numerous sophisticated aids, including a 'Technicians' Terminal' which is invaluable for testing and/or fault-finding.

The 'South' workstation main line territory extends from a boundary with Doncaster power box south of Templehirst up to and including York station. Also included are short stretches of other lines adjacent to Templehirst, Hambleton and Colton Junctions, together with the York station end of the Scarborough branch. The area controlled by the 'North' workstation takes in the main line from just north of York station (including York Yards) to a boundary with Tyneside IECC a short distance north of Northallerton. Additionally, other portions of line adjoining the ECML are controlled such as the end of the Harrogate branch at Skelton, and the low level route at Northallerton.

IECC was developed jointly by CAP Industry Ltd (now part of the Sema group) and BR (from an original BR Research concept); it has built new systems on to the Solid State Interlocking (SSI) previously adopted by BR as standard practice for new installations. With SSI, the need for massive relay rooms (like that for the superseded York box) has disappeared, and the interlocking function is carried out using electronic devices and control software which take up far less space than conventional relays. Developed as an electronic replacement for the electro-mechanical relay-based signalling technology, SSI ensures that a signal can only be cleared when the route is correctly set and the conditions are safe. The centralised control system consists of three micro-computer interlocking modules which check one another and automatically shut down any which are faulty. It is connected to solid state lineside units which operate and monitor lineside equipment, such as points and signals, and the total system provides an exact equivalent to the traditional standards of safety and reliability at lower cost.

The new installation at York has a total of eight separate interlockings; the five SSIs which cover the territory from York to Northallerton interface with the three for the southern end of the area at Templehirst, Hambleton and Colton (ie the 'Selby Diversion'), which are of the remote relay interlocking (RRI) type being relatively new equipment installed as recently as 1983.

Similar installations are to be found at Yoker (North Glasgow), Liverpool Street and Marylebone (London) and, of course, at Tyneside (Gateshead). New developments include IECC installations planned for Manchester and Liverpool, on the Great Western main line out of Paddington (which is going to be controlled by a IECC at Slough), and further extensions to the Liverpool Street scheme. In the longer term it is even anticipated that the two massive power boxes at Birmingham (New Street and Saltley) may eventually be replaced by one IECC – subject, as always, to the constraints of finance and technical resources.

Admittedly, the Liverpool Street and Yoker schemes preceded that at York; but it has to be said, with some pride, that the York remodelling and resignalling for electrification was the first IECC scheme to encompass both a large through passenger station *and* a 50-odd mile section of a busy important main line.

A century of change indeed!

Above right:
Another undated Treacy photograph (probably taken in the early 1950s) of a down express hauled by 'V2' No 60864 passing Castle Hills just north of Northallerton. The outside tracks are the former Castle Hills-Wiske Moor loops, and the track to the right of the train was the Castle Hills Reversing Line which formed the only access to the Redmire branch. *E. Treacy*

Right:
Although strictly speaking beyond the subject matter of this book, it was thought that a picture of the end of the line at Redmire might be appropriate seeing that York IECC controlled trains on and off the branch! Here on 3 July 1989, Class 37s Nos 37517 and 37518 are shunting in Redmire Tarmac sidings with the daily freight train from Redcar. *BR*

8. 1961-1991 - Three Decades of Transition: Steam to Electrics

During the mid-1950s the British Transport Commission (BTC) 'Modernisation Plan' began to gather momentum, and in his report dated December 1954 the Chairman, Sir Brian Robertson, foreshadowed the demise of steam traction in favour of electric and diesel locomotives and/or multiple units. He proposed, among other things, electrification of the ECML from 'King's Cross to Doncaster and Leeds and (possibly) York'. Subsequently, a Government White Paper (Cmd 813) published in 1959 contained a reappraisal of the 1955 Modernisation Plan which said that only one of the two main routes proposed for electrification would now be progressed – the West Coast Main Line (WCML) between London (Euston) and Birmingham/ Crewe/Manchester and Liverpool (which eventually became operative on 18 April 1966) – and the King's Cross-Leeds ('and possibly York') scheme for the ECML would be put back (quote) to 'sometime after 1964'!

Incidentally, the same White Paper formally recognised the BTC's decision to henceforth adopt 25kV as standard for future electrification.

The scene was set, therefore, for the introduction of diesel traction on the ECML, and the first locomotives to become available were the English Electric 2,000hp Type 4s – better known as the Class 40s – which appeared on some main line trains serving York during 1958/59. The diesels in their early days were not always reliable, one of the main difficulties being the train heating boiler, and it was not uncommon for a Pacific – particularly one in fairly good condition with an enthusiastic fireman and reasonable quality coal – to out-perform the Class 40s. In fact, right up to introduction of the 'Deltics' in 1961/62, steam enjoyed a kind of 'Indian summer' on the ECML.

Nevertheless, as things improved, diesel locomotives gradually took over the Newcastle-Liverpool and Newcastle-Bristol expresses.

Above:
A King's Cross-Newcastle express in charge of Deltic D9003 pauses at York station Platform 5 (9) on 2 May 1964.
J. S. Whiteley

Anticipating that the days of steam were numbered, English Electric took a bold step and, at their own expense, built a new high powered prototype diesel locomotive known as the 'Deltic'.

This remarkable machine, its Napier engines being a development of those used on Royal Navy coastal patrol boats, was way ahead of the other competitors in the field. Designed for sustained running at speeds of up to 100 mph, the prototype (not viewed with much enthusiasm by the London Midland Region to whom it had been offered in the first instance) was tried for clearances at York, and many other ECML locations, during 1959. Then, on a specially arranged trial run with 10 coaches plus dynamometer car from King's Cross to Newcastle which took place on 15 March 1959, the prototype 'Deltic' (driven by the legendary King's Cross driver Bill

Hoole) ran the 268 miles in 236 minutes – four minutes faster than the prewar 'Silver Jubilee' – and the significance of this feat was not lost upon the East Coast management of the day. The redoubtable Gerry Fiennes in particular recognised the potential of the 'Deltic' as the ideal candidate to bridge the gap until electrification (whenever that was going to be), and much of the credit must rest with him for the foresight, drive and initiative he displayed in order to secure a 22-strong fleet of 'Deltics' which would transform the principal ECML services.

With 3,300hp 'under the bonnet', the

'Deltics' (or Class 55s as they became known) were gradually delivered between February 1961 and May 1962, and they soon became a familiar sight at York – though at that time none of them was allocated to York shed. The fleet was shared out between Finsbury Park, Gateshead and Edinburgh (Haymarket) depots, and drastic cuts were made to the schedules for the 1962 summer timetable. Something just over six hours soon became the norm for the overall journey time between King's Cross and Edinburgh – not that much different from the prewar 'Coronation'!

Nevertheless, despite the timing improvements gained, the full speed potential of the 'Deltics' could not be exploited until civil engineering improvements were effected at many locations. For example, in the late 1960s only 95 miles out of the total 393 miles from London to Edinburgh was fit for 100 mph running. However, this problem was energetically tackled to the extent that by May 1978 the figure had risen to 260 miles (by then in readiness for the High Speed Train era).

Once the Deltics were established on the 'best' ECML services, the Class 40s moved on to other kinds of work. Interestingly, a York-allocated Class 40 was diagrammed right through to Inverness and back with the 'Car Sleeper' service (later called 'Motorail') – something previously unheard of, and impossible anyway, in the days of steam. As diesel locomotives of many kinds, along with DMUs on local services, were increasing-ly seen in and around York during the early/mid-1960s, the inevitable end of steam drew near, and (officially at any rate) 1965 was the last year for steam on the ECML. To commemorate the occasion, a steam-hauled relief train, with Class A1 No 60145 *Saint Mungo* at the front, was run from York to Newcastle and back to signify the event.

Actually, No 60145 was one of two emergency Pacifics stationed at Darlington, and after the closure of Darlington shed on 27 March 1966 it was allocated to York between 17 April and its final withdrawal on 19 June 1966.

Steam returned to York during the 1970s and several preserved locomotives could often be seen on a variety of special trains (as demonstrated by some of the photographs herein). The 1980s saw the introduction of the 'Scarborough Spa Express', a BR sponsored initiative, which actually did a circular tour York-Leeds-Harrogate-York-Scarborough-York. One attraction of these seasonal trains was the variety of motive power, and BR in conjunction with the local council at Scarborough installed a turntable on the site of the former Scarborough MPD. (This had become a necessity because the triangular turning facility at Filey Holiday Camp station ceased to be available after 1977.)

Patronage of the 'Scarborough Spa Express' service declined during 1987, and in the event 1988 was the last summer of regular steam excursions operation at York. Now the ECML is electrified, steam hauled specials are no longer encouraged at York station – though the occasional movement of NRM locomotives in steam (plus support coach) still takes place from time to time.

The upper limits of 'Deltic' performance were reached during the early 1970s, and while the potential for track and signalling improvements had not yet been realised to the full, it became obvious that only a new form of traction would sustain the momentum on the ECML otherwise all the advantages gained so far would soon be dissipated. Moreover, the introduction of the Class 47s into ECML workings – a good machine but hardly a match for the 'Deltics' when it came to hard running – tended to cause problems for planners, operators and marketing men alike.

Despite the extension of WCML electrification through to Glasgow (Central) completed in 1974, there was still no firm commitment forthcoming from Government circles towards electrifying the ECML; so, the new form of traction was the High Speed Train (HST) – better known as InterCity 125 – and there can be no doubt that with their two power

Below:
Steam was still active in 1965, and in this picture which does much to emphasise the excellence of the station roof, 'B1' 61319 pauses at Platform 5 (9) with the 09.21 (Saturdays only) Huddersfield-Scarborough on 19 June 1965. *B. L. Jenkins*

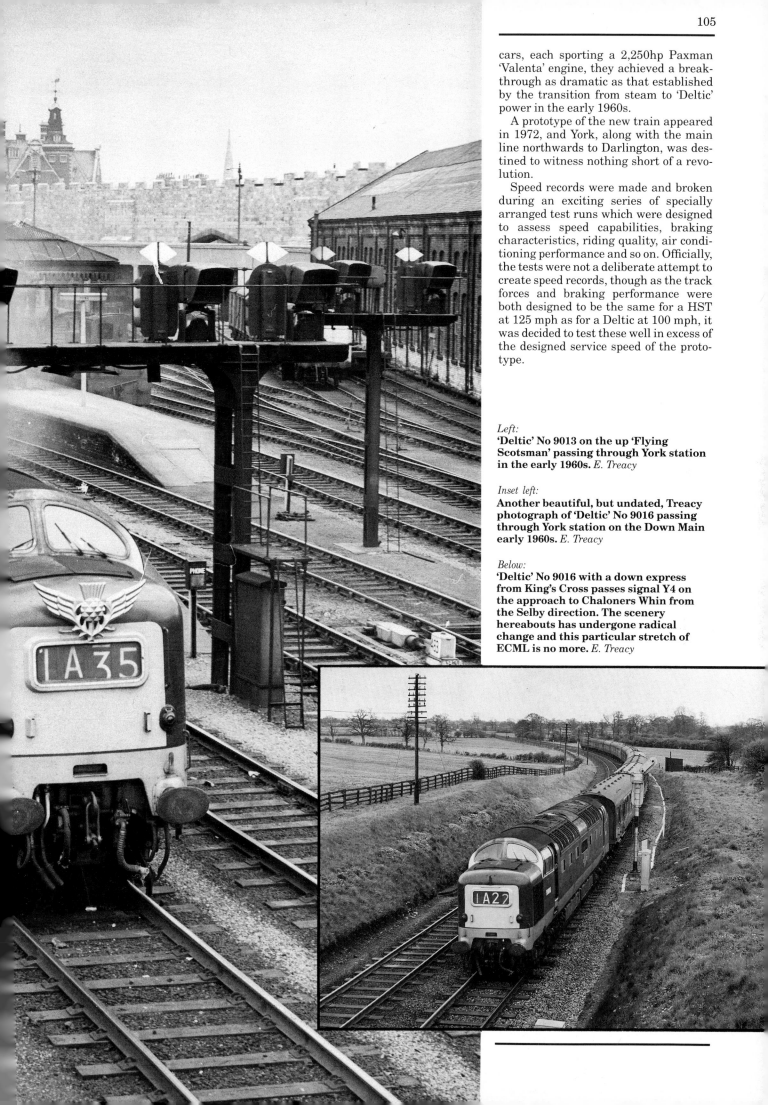

cars, each sporting a 2,250hp Paxman 'Valenta' engine, they achieved a breakthrough as dramatic as that established by the transition from steam to 'Deltic' power in the early 1960s.

A prototype of the new train appeared in 1972, and York, along with the main line northwards to Darlington, was destined to witness nothing short of a revolution.

Speed records were made and broken during an exciting series of specially arranged test runs which were designed to assess speed capabilities, braking characteristics, riding quality, air conditioning performance and so on. Officially, the tests were not a deliberate attempt to create speed records, though as the track forces and braking performance were both designed to be the same for a HST at 125 mph as for a Deltic at 100 mph, it was decided to test these well in excess of the designed service speed of the prototype.

Left:
'Deltic' No 9013 on the up 'Flying Scotsman' passing through York station in the early 1960s. *E. Treacy*

Inset left:
Another beautiful, but undated, Treacy photograph of 'Deltic' No 9016 passing through York station on the Down Main early 1960s. *E. Treacy*

Below:
'Deltic' No 9016 with a down express from King's Cross passes signal Y4 on the approach to Chaloners Whin from the Selby direction. The scenery hereabouts has undergone radical change and this particular stretch of ECML is no more. *E. Treacy*

Left:
A different diesel locomotive this time. English Electric Class 20 No 8308 leaving York Platform 6 (10) with the 17.08 to Hull on 29 August 1970.
D. Wharton

Below:
Steam returned with a vengeance! Midland compound No 1000 lays a smokescreen over York as it leaves with a private charter train for Rochdale on 28 September 1983. *B. Dobbs*

Above:
Mallard **in all its glory again (courtesy of the Friends of the NRM), arriving at York Platform 5 (9) on 9 July 1986.** *BR*

Above right:
Another shot of ***Mallard*,** **this time leaving York bound for Scarborough on 9 July 1986. The train is passing over 'Scarborough Bridge' which spans the River Ouse shortly after departure from York station.** *BR*

Right:
The power and the majesty of steam is captured in this picture of '9F' 2-10-0 No 92220 ***Evening Star*** **at Platform 5 (9) on 9 August 1983. This was the last main line steam locomotive to be built by BR and was completed in 1960.** *BR*

This culminated in a series of spectacular runs in June 1973 when the train was reduced to 2+5 formation. Special instrumentation was used on board as well as at certain selected places along the line, and comprehensive operating procedures were drawn up to allow running at above the permitted line speed – especially to safeguard the position at occupation crossings, four of which were encountered within a few miles between Thirsk and Northallerton. The test trains were not allowed to leave either York or Darlington, until a specific assurance had been obtained via a District Inspector located in York box for the purpose of co-ordinating the arrangements that everything en-route was as it should be. Thus, on 6 June 1973 a speed of 131 mph was attained going north – beating the 'Mallard record of 1938' by 5 mph. Then on 12 June 1973, this time going south, a speed of 141 mph was reached near Thirsk – so eclipsing the 1939 record of 133 mph held by Germany's 'Flying Hamburger'.

However, on the same day, the prototype twice reached a new maximum when 143.2 mph was recorded going north at MP 25¼ beyond Thirsk, and on a subsequent run this new record was

Right:
InterCity 125 set No 254031 leaving York Platform 3 (8) with the 09.15 Edinburgh-King's Cross train on 7 April 1980, while 'Deltic' No 55008 *The Green Howards* awaits departure in Platform 1 (3) with the 12.15 semi-fast York-King's Cross service. *J. E. Oxley*

Centre right:
Another shot of the prototype HST, this time taken on 6 June 1973 at Holgate Bridge en route for Neville Hill after completion of the day's work. Earlier the same day, the train had achieved a speed of 131mph, thus breaking the record held by *Mallard* since 1938. Nevertheless, the prototype HST was soon to improve upon its own performance and break further speed records later that month! *N. E. Preedy*

Left:
No self-respecting book about York's railways should miss out a shot of No 46229 *Duchess of Hamilton*. Here the famous locomotive is seen making a spectacular departure from Platform 10 (15) with a FNRM sponsored steam special on 10 May 1980. *BR*

Below left:
Class 47 No 47541 coming round the 'Severus Curve' heading northwards with the 11.00 King's Cross-Newcastle service on 21 September 1975. *L. A. Nixon*

Below:
The prototype HST rolls into York station on 11 June 1973 upon completion of yet another high speed test run. However, no records were broken on 11 June, though on the following day a maximum of 141mph was achieved southbound near Thirsk. *BR*

reached for a second time at MP 28 north of Otterington in the course of maintaining an average of more than 140 mph over a distance of 12 miles.

All this demonstrated what could be done safely, and by the end of 1974 Government approval was given for the construction of 32 HST sets for the ECML. Actually, the Eastern Region had made out a conclusive case for 42 sets – but, as ever, someone somewhere else knew better. In the event, the Western Region got in first, and BR's first batch of Inter-City 125s entered service on the London (Paddington)-Bristol-South Wales route, taking 22min off the Paddington-Bristol schedule at one stroke. So the ECML had, perforce, to wait until 1978; the new trains were first to be seen regularly at York from February 1978, after their

gradual introduction on existing 100 mph timings.

By early 1979, plans were firmed up for a marketing launch –accompanied by media publicity – to coincide with the introduction of a completely new summer timetable on 14 May 1979.

It was envisaged that York would benefit from faster and more frequent main line trains than ever before. But, disaster struck in the early hours of 17 March 1979 during the course of overnight engineering work, when the roof of Penmanshiel Tunnel collapsed, completely blocking the ECML between Berwick and Dunbar. This prompted a decision to seal the tunnel after further rock falls had been encountered, and to bypass the site by a new railway alignment constructed alongside the neighbouring A1

trunk road, so direct services between Newcastle and Edinburgh were not resumed until 20 August 1979.

Thereafter, the HST era settled down, and subsequently InterCity 125s were introduced into other important services. For instance, by the end of 1981 it was possible to travel direct from York to Paignton or Penzance by HST. By 1984, most of the Cross Country NE/SW HST services had been re-routed to travel via Doncaster, apart from a few which ran via Leeds, and another innovation was the successful King's Cross-Inverness train, and vice-versa, which still offers through journeys between York and previously unheard of destinations (a much appreciated facility).

It is a fair assumption that without the HST the InterCity business might well have died on its feet long ago (or drifted into the doldrums – rather like the West Coast main line seems to have done at the present time through no particular fault of its own). In fact, it is probably the most successful 125 mph diesel train in the world – and certainly the most hard worked.

Nonetheless, after all these years, the HST is still overall an attractive proposition (and putting in considerably more mileage than originally thought).

Another speed exploit worthy of mention is a further record established not very far from Essendine where *Mallard* did 126 mph running downhill from Stoke summit on 3 July 1938. On 27 September 1985, to commemorate the passage of 50 years since the Press Run of the 'Silver Jubilee' and also the 10th anniversary of the National Railway Museum's opening, a relaunched 'Tyne-Tees' Pullman train, specially reduced to 2+5 formation, achieved yet another record of 144 mph around MP 90, and just for good measure on the way back from King's Cross, the same train accelerated to 126 mph, this time going *up*

Top left:
Distance no object by courtesy of InterCity 125. By the time this photograph was taken in September 1977, the overall journey time between the two capital cities had been reduced to below that of the prewar 'Coronation'. Here No 245001 races south past the 'half-way' sign between Tollerton and Beningbrough. *BR*

Centre left:
Another classic location shot from the HST era taken in April 1979 heading northwards from York. *BR*

Left:
Slow and fast services side by side on 13 April 1982. In the foreground No 43077 awaits departure from Platform 6 (10) with the 14.15 semi-fast York-King's Cross service, whilst in the background No 43080 departs with the 08.35 Aberdeen-King's Cross train. The semi-fast will leave 10min after the up Aberdeen service but arrive in London 1hr 6min later! *J. E. Oxley*

Stoke bank!, which demonstrated the InterCity 125s real worth in no uncertain manner.

In the meantime, 1982 saw the end of the 'Deltic' era. 19 out of the 22 strong fleet finished their working days based at York shed, many of them being used on the Liverpool services. (It was quite a sight to see – and hear – a 'Deltic' trailing a cloud of blue smoke behind it while throbbing its way out of Lime Street station through the tunnels going up to Edge Hill.) The three 'Deltics' left at Finsbury Park were withdrawn during 1980, followed by 16 of the York allocation during 1981. Finally, the last three Deltics were taken out of traffic on 3 January 1982 and yet another chapter of ECML locomotive history came to an end.

And so, at long last, main line electrification came to York! Authorised in 1984,

Top:
Diverted via York Yards due to weekday engineering work at the north end of York station (which included renewal of the 'Clifton Diamonds'), the up 'Flying Scotsman' passes York Yard South on Thursday 8 April 1981. *A. Taylor*

Above:
The high-speed InterCity 225 nonstop test run from King's Cross to Edinburgh passes the 'half way' sign between Beningbrough and Tollerton on 26 September 1991. *BR*

and extended from Edinburgh to Glasgow Central (to Carstairs actually) in September 1989, the first stage of the ECML electrification was completed between King's Cross and Leeds during 1989, and electric hauled services were gradually phased in. The first overhead

line mast was erected at Peterborough on 7 February 1985, and exactly two years later on 7 February 1987, the 12,000th mast was ceremoniously put in place at York station – adjacent to the buffer stops at Platform 1 (3) – by the then Prime Minister (Mrs Margaret Thatcher) to mark the start of work in the York area. The first electric locomotive to have the distinction of running under its own power at York was No 91010, which was used during the testing of overhead line equipment on 17 September 1989, and the first to actually work a train was No 91003 which took a 1G50 special to London on Saturday 23 September 1989.

Yet another speed record surely deserves a mention. During some specially arranged tests to observe, among other things, the behaviour of the pantograph, Class 91 No 91010 attained a

The original authority was for 31 new trains, each set consisting of a Class 91 electric Bo-Bo 6,300hp locomotive, eight Mark 4 vehicles and a Driver Van Trailer (DVT), but a later supplementary approval was forthcoming for the provision of an extra 31 coaches to cater for the steadily rising passenger loadings stimulated by the journey time reductions brought about by the HSTs.

In practice, the trains usually operate with the locomotive leading northwards from King's Cross, and the DVT leading going south. Control of the train, when the DVT is leading, is by means of Time Division Multiplex (TDM) equipment which is designed to feed low-voltage pulses along the train's internal wiring system, so that the driver's commands (from his driving position in the DVT) are transmitted instantaneously to the locomotive. In appearance a complete IC225 train presents a sleek, exciting and modern image – a worthy successor to the IC125 – and some of the 'best' services are now down to around $1^{3}/_{4}$ hr journey time between York and London. Whilst the design speed capability caters for running at a maximum of 140 mph (225 k/ph), this cannot yet be exploited unless a radically different signalling system is introduced – doubtless accompanied by Automatic Train Protection (ATP) – so the electrics operate at an upper speed of 125 mph.

Electric operation north of York commenced with the July 1991 timetable (following the completion of the Newcastle resignalling), and an augmented service applied from October 1991. A further revised service was introduced in May 1992; currently the timetable provides for something like 75% electrics and 25% HSTs on the ECML, with no scheduled Class 47 haulage. As the additional coaches were delivered, and the formations increased to 2+9, some HSTs have been 'cascaded' to other routes within the InterCity business.

Finally, the important role played by Provincial – now Regional Railways – in the development of passenger train services at York must not be underestimated. Both journey opportunities and overall timings have been improved – in some cases out of all recognition – within the past two or three years, as will be seen from a survey of the present day scene which appears in Chapter 9.

speed of 161.7 mph on Sunday 17 September 1990 while going down Stoke bank. This time the highest speed was reached at MP 87½ between Essendine and Tallington, a couple of miles or so south of where *Mallard* did 126 mph in 1938. However, the absolute upper speed reached by any kind of train on BR was achieved by the prototype Advanced Passenger Train (APT) on the WCML between Beattock and Lockerbie on 20 December 1979 – an amazing 162.2 mph.

Another literally amazing and even more spectacular exploit, conducted recently, was a specially arranged nonstop run from King's Cross to Edinburgh. 140 mph running was permitted for this one occasion, and specific operating procedures were drawn up so that a clear road was virtually assured in the interests of safety. On Thursday 26 September 1991, a Class 91 locomotive plus five coaches and DVT was booked to leave King's Cross at 09.00, and the planned passing times of 10.00 at Newark Northgate, 11.00 at Ferryhill and 12.00 just over the border at Reston, with a scheduled arrival time of 12.29 at Edinburgh Waverley really makes one think. On the day, things worked out remarkably well, and a planned timing of 1hr 33min from King's Cross to York took some believing – until it actually happened. Needless to say, the return journey with intermediate stops at Newcastle, York and Peterborough was made in a much more sedate fashion!

9. Towards the 21st Century - York's Modern Railway System

To bring the York railway story right up to the present day, it has to be said that the whole scenario has recently undergone significant changes. Things are vastly different from how they used to be. Not only has the infrastructure taken on a new look, due mainly to the remodelling of track layouts and electrification, but the train services provided by both InterCity and Regional Railways have been completely transformed.

It is particularly noticeable too that many previously unheard of journey opportunities have been created due to recent train service revisions; long established ways of running the railway have altered as well. The most recent reorganisation – 'Organising for Quality' – has an avowed objective of ensuring the adoption of a much more businesslike approach than hitherto in the overall conduct of railway affairs, together with renewed emphasis focused upon safety, quality of service and customer care.

York Station Today

York station still looks as impressive as ever, especially so since the latest improvements which were carried out during 1983/84 and culminated in the opening of a new Travel Centre, complete with a Telephone Enquiry Bureau containing the most up to date equipment designed to minimise waiting time for callers.

The scheme also included resurfacing the floor of both the inner and outer concourses with 'terrazzo' tiles, and the provision of a new waiting room on

Above right:
York's modern railway at work: (1) a northbound HST is coming round the 'Severus Curve' shortly after leaving York on 26 June 1991. *BR*

Right:
York's modern railway at work: (2) a southbound InterCity 225 is rounding the 'Severus Curve' on its way towards York station on 26 June 1991. *BR*

Left:
Platform box is the only one of the manual boxes displaced in the 1951 resignalling to survive. This is the rear view taken from the inner concourse on 6 August 1992. The end nearest the camera is now the Duty Station Manager's office; the other end being used mainly by the 'Customer Care' staff. *Mrs C. A. Appleby*

Below left:
Ancient and modern under York station roof, on 28 May 1988. 'Sprinter' No 150260 forming the 10.01 Liverpool Lime Street-Scarborough service is seen against the NER cast mural on one of the roof supports. *Brian Morrison*

Below:
The preserved NER semaphore signal forms the centre piece of York station's revitalised outer concourse, taken in November 1984 with the new Travel Centre in the background. *BR*

Platform 3 (8). Complete restoration of the 1942 air-raid damage was also undertaken. Then in 1985 York became an 'open' station, and the ticket barriers were removed following the introduction of a comprehensive on-train ticket examination system.

When electrification came along, a few problems arose because York station is a listed building. Not only had the consent of the appropriate local authority to be obtained before any alterations could be made, but the approval of the Royal Fine Art Commission was also needed. One of the main causes for concern was how to find the best way to fit supports for the overhead wires as unobtrusively as possible within the central part of the main trainshed. The preferred solution was to sling the wires from existing pillars, rather than masts, and one can but say that the result is aesthetically pleasing.

The vast quantities of parcels traffic, parcels post and newspapers, once commonplace at York station – particularly during the night – have gone for ever, though 'Red Star' traffic is still dealt with. A few locomotive-hauled parcels trains are still to be seen, these being provided for the conveyance of letter mail under the new 'brand name' Rail Express Systems (RES).

Similarly, the maintenance and cleaning of coaching stock vehicles at Clifton Carriage Sidings, where extensive modernisation of facilities was undertaken

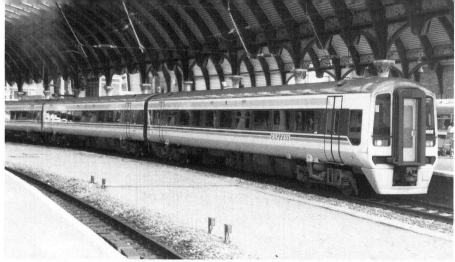

as recently as during 1983, was only destined to last for some four years after a redefined long term strategy for the fleet decreed that there was no longer a future for Clifton depot. The site has since been cleared and given over to what a large notice-board describes as a 'prestigious housing development'. (Since the closure of Clifton depot some six years ago, it is now customary to clean the overnight standage of DMUs in the bay platforms at York station.)

The nature of motive power and train crew activities at York has also undergone dramatic change in recent years. As InterCity services have been accelerated, justification for the continued involvement of York crews in long distance workings (eg, to London) has now disappeared, and for much the same reason their freight workings have also been curtailed. York train crews are now mainly employed on Regional Railways passenger services.

InterCity Train Services

The range of InterCity train services currently available to customers wishing to travel to or from York represents a great improvement compared with the not too distant past. For instance, on the ECML the Monday-Friday service operative from 14 May 1992 offers a total of 27 trains to King's Cross between the hours of 06.00 and 21.40. In the reverse direction, a similar number of services provide eight trains to Glasgow Central, augmented by six to Edinburgh, with the remainder terminating at Newcastle.

York also has three through services to Aberdeen and one to Inverness which are worked by HSTs. Newcastle is particularly well served by InterCity services from York, with an overall choice of 30 trains daily. On the cross-country route, there is a variety of 13 regular daily departures – mostly HSTs but there are still a few locomotive-hauled trains – plus two summer season Friday night

Below:

The simplified York south end track layout is seen on 6 August 1992, as an InterCity 125 runs towards Platform 5 (9) parallel with a Liverpool-Newcastle 158 proceeding into Platform 10 (15). *Mrs C. A. Appleby*

Left:
Compare this present-day scene at York south end with many of the other similar location photographs taken over the years! Here an InterCity 225 heads south from Platform 3 (8) on 6 August 1992. *Mrs C. A. Appleby*

trains, one to Penzance and the other to Paignton.

Through journeys can be made from York to destinations such as Bristol, Plymouth, Penzance, Bournemouth and Swansea, just to quote a few examples, and there is even a through train to Paddington at 14.07 which runs via Birmingham and Oxford.

Since 1984, most NE/SW services to and from the York direction are now routed via Doncaster, though a few run via Leeds and the southern end of the ex-S&K joint line via the South Kirby-Moorthorpe curve.

Incidentally, only three InterCity trains are now scheduled to pass York station without stopping; two Pullman services from Newcastle go through at 07.29 and 07.57 in the up direction, and on the down line only the 17.00 King's Cross-Edinburgh misses out York when it passes by at 18.44. The fact that two of the prestigious morning services do not call is of little consequence as York has its own starting train at 07.40 – the 'White Rose Pullman'.

Regional Railways Train Services

In recent years, Regional Railways NorthEast has made strenuous efforts to improve both the image and appeal of their services on secondary lines radiating from York (with the solitary exception of the York-Sheffield local DMU service via the S&K route).

The most significant improvements are evident on the TransPennine route between Newcastle (and Middlesbrough from 14 May 1992) to Liverpool via Manchester Piccadilly, where a total of 15 Express services operate from York on weekdays (between 06.32 and 20.33). Of these, seven trains to Liverpool are from Newcastle, five from Middlesbrough, two start from York and one (the 07.36 departure) is a combination of Newcastle and Middlesbrough portions. Additionally, these services are augmented by 11 other fast trains to Manchester Piccadilly,

most of which originate at Scarborough.

This completely revitalised TransPennine business is sponsored by Regional Railways NorthEast, even though part of the route is in Regional Railways North-West territory, and there can be little doubt as to its overall success. Operated by 90 mph Class 158 DMUs (the earlier technical problems now seem to be cured following certain modifications), a fast, frequent journey – in air conditioned comfort – now puts Manchester and Liverpool within 90 and 141min respectively of York. The 90 mph capability of the Class 158s, coupled with various permanent way upgradings at a number of critical locations *en route,* has enabled line speeds to be raised in order to provide this much enhanced service. The Scarborough-Manchester trains are also operated by Class 158 Express DMUs, and even though they make a couple of additional stops, they too reach Manchester from York in around 92min!

By May 1993 it is anticipated that the projected new rail link direct into Manchester Airport will become available, in which case the Scarborough-Manchester trains are to be extended beyond Piccadilly to form a through service from York. In fact, TransPennine is now so important as to warrant serious consideration being given to an electrification strategy which, if carried through, could result in a link up between the ECML and WCML electrified systems at both Manchester and Liverpool. However, it is early days yet, and funding problems for such projects inevitably become more and more difficult in this day and age – but it is an interesting prospect.

There is also the alternative service from York to Manchester to consider which operates via Leeds, Bradford Interchange (reverse) and Halifax, to join the former L&Y main line at Milner Royd Junction near Sowerby Bridge. (There used to be a York-Sowerby Bridge service via Normanton and Wakefield until 1970.) Trains run from York at regular intervals throughout the day, calling at all or most intermediate stations

(according to whether one travels on a xx23 or xx48 service), and a total of 26 services are on offer between 07.00 and 21.48 on weekdays. Twelve xx23 trains terminate at Manchester Victoria, another 12 xx48 trains go forward to Liverpool (calling at all stations) and two run to Halifax only. Understandably, these services (marketed as the 'Calder Vale' line) are rather slower than the expresses via Huddersfield, so the journey time from York to Manchester takes a couple of minutes over two hours. Liverpool is reached in just over three hours this way, hence these services are announced at York (and shown on the TV screens) as only going to Edge Hill, doubtless to deter passengers who want a fast ride to Liverpool from being tempted to join.

Regional Railways also operate a fairly regular (almost hourly) service on the York-Harrogate-Leeds line, comprising 16 trains throughout the day between 06.54 and 21.37. A number of semaphore signals, together with several examples of hand worked level crossing gates can still be seen on this line – mostly between Poppleton and Harrogate – where something of the country branch line atmosphere has managed to survive. There are two single line sections signalled by Electric Key Token instruments: Poppleton-Hammerton (singled 4 June 1972); and, Cattal-Knaresborough (singled 16 December 1973). Absolute Block working, however, continues on the remaining double line sections. Poppleton is, of course, a fringe box to York IECC.

Scarborough too has an almost hourly service on normal weekdays with 15 trains from York between 07.20 and 22.10. Services on this line are augmented on Saturdays during the peak Summer season – though not to the extent to which they were up to a few years ago. Absolute Block and semaphore signals are still to be seen on this line east of Strensall, with the exception of Malton where colour lights were

Above right:
Class 47 No 47452 heads south out of York with the 08.25 Newcastle-Liverpool train on 14 May 1988. Note the newly erected IECC building to the left of the picture. *W. A. Sharman*

Right:
A rear view of the 08.03 Liverpool-Scarborough service arriving at York on 7 May 1988. Three new buildings are visible in this photograph, viz: S&T Workshops (left); Mercury Communications centre (middle); and, IECC (right). *W. A. Sharman*

installed in 1966, and much of the Scarborough branch still has the appearance of a typical NER country railway.

Strensall is the fringe box to York IECC; it now has a modern panel and controls/monitors several level crossings in the vicinity.

Various other local services are operated to Selby, Hull and Sheffield, and there is quite a variety of DMUs sporting different liveries to be seen in and around York. North of York, the intermediate ECML stations at Thirsk and Northallerton are served by the TransPennine Newcastle/Middlesbrough services, though Northallerton – the administrative heart of North Yorkshire County Council – also has a service of a few InterCity trains.

Despite the loss of certain branch lines in earlier years, the frequent 'Express' services across the Pennines, together with the fairly regular local trains represents a creditable achievement by Regional Railways, especially so in today's difficult economic situation. Although commuting by rail does not form a major part of the passenger activity at York, every now and then the question arises about reopening the closed stations at Haxby and Strensall, both of which are on the Scarborough line. Due to continual housing development over the years, what were once country villages have gradually grown almost into outer suburban dormitories, and the subject is once again under discussion between the various interested parties. Similar pleas have also been made about the possibility of reopening Copmanthorpe station for much the same reason, though the position is rather complicated because the former station site is now situated on the ECML (since the 'Selby Diversion' opened in 1983), and it seems that the many practical problems involved would very much outweigh the case for reopening.

Nevertheless, one station in the locality which has reopened in recent years is Sherburn in Elmet. Closed to passengers as long ago as 13 September 1965, Sherburn was reopened as an unstaffed halt on 9 July 1984, supposedly for a trial period of six months, and while it was originally served only by the York-Sheffield local DMU services, a further development since 14 May 1992 resulted in some (but not all) of the York-Selby/Hull DMUs being diverted off the ECML between Colton and Hambleton to run via Church Fenton and Gascoigne Wood and thus to stop at Sherburn in Elmet – yet one more example of how new journey opportunities can be created.

Rail Express Systems (RES) Train Services

The parcels business is no longer a 'mini-sector' in its own right; in 1991 it became known as the 'Parcels Group', essentially a joint venture of the four passenger businesses (ie: InterCity, Regional Railways, Network SouthEast and European Passenger Services). Originally comprised of four profit centres, namely, 'Train Load' (effectively the Post Office Contract), Red Star, Red Star International and 'Track 29', a further reorganisation during 1992 in line with 'Organising for Quality' (OFQ) but enforced by the recession which added to the problems of recovery following the loss of newspaper traffic in 1988, saw a merger of the four components into two — thus 'Train Load' absorbed 'Track 29' and Red Star overtook the International part of the business. Now carrying the brand-name 'Rail Express Systems' (RES), a fairly comprehensive network of postal (or mails) trains now covers most major centres throughout the UK, though rather like the coal for power stations mentioned elsewhere in this chapter the future is clouded with uncertainties because of rail privatisation, coupled with the fact that the current contract for the conveyance of Her Majesty's Mails by rail is up for renewal in October 1993. Yet another complication is the recently suggested privatisation of the Post Office itself!

Nevertheless, mainly during the night hours (bearing in mind that Anglo-Scottish Sleeping Car services are now concentrated on the West Coast route) a number of important RES trains — hauled by Class 47s — converge upon York, some of which convey Travelling Post Office vehicles (TPOs). Also the traditional close working relationship between BR and the Royal Mail is evidenced by the dedicated lift on Platform 4 (formerly 8B or 8 North) which affords direct access between York station and the adjacent Sorting Office on Leeman Road.

Organisation

In order to appreciate fully the local railway scene, one really needs to gain a general impression as to how and why the most recent and radical reorganisation of railway affairs affecting York developed. By tradition the various ground level activities at York were managed by a number of different local officials; thus York station was under the jurisdiction of the 'Station Master', though purely commercial matters were dealt with by a Passenger & Parcels Agent who was in charge of the Booking and Parcels Offices. The marshalling yards were the prerogative of another official known as the 'Yard Master', and the motive power depot was looked after by a 'Locomotive Shed Master' (latterly 'Depot Manager'). The goods handling and cartage functions at Leeman Road and Foss Islands freight depots were managed by a 'Goods Agent', until the freight sundries and cartage activities were overtaken by National Carriers Ltd (NCL). The various civil, signals, and mechanical engineering functions all had their own technical organisations which tended to cover a district, rather than local, sphere of activity.

Out on the line, there were Station Masters based at all medium sized and most small stations in the immediate vicinity of York. Over the years, a variety of organisational changes occurred, but probably the most significant event was the creation of an Area Management structure which, from 16 March 1970, replaced the long-standing positions of Station Masters, Yard Masters and the like. The newly appointed Area Manager (the author!) assumed command of all operating and commercial activities in an area which embraced York, Selby, Thirsk and Harrogate. Then, following yet another reorganisation, which became effective during 1975, the York Area Manager also assumed responsibility for the Scarborough line. Actually, the York Area of that time, along with the railway network in West Yorkshire, formed part of the then Leeds Division (and responded to a Divisional Manager's organisation based at Leeds).

Subsequent adjustments to Area and Divisional boundaries eventually culminated in the abolition of Divisional Managers' organisations in 1984, and finally even the York Area (which by then had grown in size by having taken over the former Hull Area) ceased to exist as a separate entity from 27 February 1989. This time, that part of the ECML in and around York became the responsibility of the Area Manager Doncaster, and the surrounding secondary routes were placed under the Area Manager Leeds.

During the early 1980s an entirely different concept of management style emerged throughout the whole of BR; the creation of 'Sectors' led to the formation of what in effect were 'individual businesses' within a corporate business. Thus the ECML through York formed part of 'InterCity', the secondary routes in the York locality became 'Provincial' – known as Regional Railways from 3 December 1990 – and the freight activities, along with parcels, were assigned to the freight and parcels sectors respectively. Effectively, a new culture had arisen, with commercial aspects henceforth known as 'business' and operational activities regarded as 'production'.

The new philosophy ultimately developed as 'Organising for Quality' (OFQ), and the final stage of this ongoing reorganisation emerged on 6 April 1992 when the Regions were disbanded. The businesses then assumed ownership of their dedicated assets and resources, together with the management and administration of all associated personnel.

The businesses have, of course, been sub-divided into self-contained fully accountable separate entities known as 'Profit Centres'. A profit centre could be defined by trunk routes – as in the case of InterCity – or by geographical and/or sensibly identifiable groups of train services on Regional Railways. The two freight businesses are rather different in that Trainload Freight is sub-divided by commodity (ie, Coal, Metals, Petroleum and Construction), whereas Railfreight Distribution has been sub-divided by activity (ie, UK and International).

Regional boundaries as such have now disappeared. Moreover, the new philosophy requires that every part of the railway infrastructure and associated resources must be 'owned' by one of the businesses, on the basis of which busi-

Left:
Changing styles of DMU: (1). The 16.39 to Harrogate stands in Platform 8 (13) on 1 October 1977. *N. A. Machell*

ness agrees it is the 'primary user' of the assets. A system of 'Trading Agreements' between the businesses then ensures that secondary and minor users' rights of access are safeguarded, subject to their making an appropriate financial contribution to the 'owner'.

York station and the ECML from King's Cross to Edinburgh Waverley (and onwards to Glasgow Central via Carstairs) is now 'owned' by InterCity – though Edinburgh Waverley and Glasgow Central stations are 'owned' by ScotRail! The various secondary routes which form most of the local rail network around York, together with the passenger stations at such places as Selby, Church Fenton, Thirsk, Northallerton, Malton and Scarborough belong to Regional Railways NorthEast. The remaining freight lines at York and Selby, together with the Redmire branch and the line from Northallerton to Eaglescliffe (which now carries a Liverpool-Middlesbrough passenger service), are the property of Trainload Freight (who also looks after the interests of the other freight business – Railfreight Distribution – on an agency basis).

Another feature relative to the two passenger businesses is the distinction now drawn between 'Retail' and 'Operations'. The term 'Retail' applies to personnel and activities which interface with customers; so staff employed in Travel Centres, Ticket Offices, on station platforms and on trains are designated 'Retail'. Thus Senior Conductors (InterCity) and Conductors (Regional Railways) – better known as 'Guards' to many people – are 'Retail' staff. On the other hand, the 'Operations' function – ie, without direct customer interface – involves all safety-related activities, such as driving trains, signalling and shunting, and staff designated as 'Operations' are required to possess a high standard of competency in operational and/or traction procedures, rules and regulations, safety related matters and the like.

Area Managers on the passenger side have been replaced by separate 'Retail' and 'Operations' organisations which specialise within their own particular fields of activity, though in the case of Trainload Freight an Area Management

structure has been retained – thus the few freight operations staff who remain at York now respond to the Area Manager (Yorkshire Freight) based at Doncaster. Concurrently with this latest reorganisation, the various engineering and technical functions have also been restructured to respond to an appropriate business.

Another point to be borne in mind is that Regional Railways derives income from Passenger Transport Executives (PTEs) and Public Service Obligation (PSO) contracts, and is therefore essentially a 'social' railway in contrast to InterCity (a 'commercial' railway) which must pay its own way since the support it once received from Government sources was discontinued after 1 April 1988.

Also, since the Regions were abolished recently, the Settle-Carlisle line – formerly in the London Midland Region – now belongs to Regional Railways NorthEast.

Finally, there have been far-reaching changes affecting the Headquarters Offices in York ; the time-honoured title of 'General Manager' ceased to exist after 6 April 1992 as a result of the foregoing organisational changes. Nonetheless, a strong presence is still maintained at York: InterCity East Coast (ECML) and Regional Railways NorthEast both have their top management and supporting staff based here, and so has Trainload Freight.

Thus the long established tradition of having a railway headquarters organisation based in York, originated by the Y&NM, expanded by the NER, perpetuated by the LNER (NE Area) and further developed by BR is set to continue – albeit in a different form! It is indeed good to know that such architecturally imposing buildings as the former 'old' station and the main headquarters offices of 1906 are to remain in railway use for the foreseeable future.

Left:
**The modern freight railway at its best!
An immaculate Class 60, No 60004 at
York Yard North on 26 June 1991 with a
down train of empty MGR wagons.** *BR*

Below left:
Selby Coalfield. *Author's Collection*

The Freight Scene

There is still quite a lot of freight train
activity to be seen in and around York.
Whilst marshalling, in the accepted
sense of the word, has been eliminated –
busy night shifts shunting at Dringhouses Yard are now but a distant memory! –
and such commercial freight business
local to York that existed up to recent
years has ceased to pass by rail, the
number of through train load freight
workings which either pass York without
stopping, or alternatively make just a
momentary call to change crews, usually
at York Yard South, have tended to
increase. This is despite the demise of
traditional wagon load services, and the
virtual disappearance of Speedlink,
accompanied by a reduction in Freightliner trains.

Furthermore, a sizeable requirement
exists at the present time for MGR coal
trains from the north (which are bound
for the Aire Valley power stations at
Drax, Eggborough and Ferrybridge),
along with the corresponding return flow
of empty MGR wagons, to be staged at
York for the purpose of changing locomotives and train crews.

This operation usually takes place in
the Up Arrival or Down Departure lines
which are situated between York Yard
North and Skelton, or alternatively in
the Up Yard, according to the availability of siding accommodation. These trains
originate at certain collieries and/or
opencast centralised disposal points in
the Durham coalfield, also from a Scottish opencast site at Ravenstruther
(located on the WCML near Carstairs).
The Scottish coal is staged at Millerhill
and Tyne Yard for crew change purposes,
and recently another flow has commenced to pass for Ironbridge power station, which is staged at York to be
worked forward via Toton.

The proportion of coal tonnages con-
veyed from the north, relative to the total
intake of the Aire Valley power stations,
is subject to a considerable degree of var-
iation hence trains run according to a
weekly programme. Similarly, the overall
intake of the three power stations themselves fluctuates to a greater or lesser
degree, according to the tonnage and
source allocations determined between
National Power (Drax and Eggborough),
PowerGen (Ferrybridge) and British Coal
– in conjunction with BR Trainload
Freight – which in turn permits a comprehensive weekly train plan to be formulat-
ed. MGR workings for the three Aire
Valley power stations are mainly the pre-

rogative of Knottingley depot. The following figures demonstrate the variable nature of the MGR operation as a whole: for week ended 21 March 1992, out of a total intake of 412,400 tonnes the proportion from the north staged at York amounted to 57,400 tonnes, whereas during week ended 18 July 92, a gross total of 248,700 tonnes required rail conveyance from the north of 95,900 tonnes! Another feature of interest, although not directly concerned with the York freight scene, is the Selby coalfield to the south.

The Selby complex covers a wide area. Coal from five separate mines (ie, North Selby (Escrick), Riccall, Stillingfleet, Whitemoor and Wistow) all interlinked beneath ground, comes to the surface at Gascoigne Wood loading terminal which is built on the site of the former Gascoigne Wood marshalling yard which closed in 1959. Two large bunkers for direct loading into MGR wagons, and a rather smaller third bunker for loading stone spoil, accompanied by a siding layout designed specially to allow a steady flow of MGR trains through the plant, provide adequate facilities for planned half-hourly departures round the clock.

MGR trains conveying coal for power stations is big business – both nationally and locally for Trainload Freight, thus the fluctuating volume of long-haul coal traffic staged through York, together with the high-tonnage short-haul operation within the Yorkshire coalfield in general, and the Selby coalfield in particular, is of significant importance. Indeed, to quote from a jointly sponsored NCB/CEGB/BR news sheet published 10 years ago, entitled *Selby Enterprise,* the then new ECML and Selby coalfield projects, and the impending construction of a second 20 megawatt power station at Drax, between them '...provided a good illustration of how the three nationalised industries could work closely together to provide an efficient and economic supply of power for the nation'. Moreover, at that time, there was no doubt that the MGR concept was both a logistically sensible and an environmentally-friendly method of moving large tonnages of coal for power stations. However, subsequent privatisation of electricity generation heralded change in that Drax and Eggborough power stations now form part of National Power, whereas Ferrybridge belongs to PowerGen, and problems have since been encountered concerning the three year contract between British Coal and the two privatised power generating companies, which is up for renewal in April 1993. Obviously this has given rise to concern, both in the coal industry and on BR, accompanied (as usual) by rumour and speculation. Much has been said in the media about the electricity generators apparently wishing to import large tonnages of allegedly cheap coal from abroad (supposedly of low sulphur content too), which could have an adverse effect upon the freight scene at York. Also, according to a contemporary report in York's local evening newspaper, National Power was even said to be considering construction of a canal from the Selby coalfield to Drax and Eggborough! The same source quoted PowerGen as having expressed an intention to reduce the amount of coal intake by rail at Ferrybridge.

Such extreme ideas may prove to be groundless, though it seems likely that by the time this book appears in print perhaps a tough demanding contract (of reduced tonnage?) will have been hammered out between the parties concerned. Whether or not the freight scene at York will continue much as described herein still remains to be seen, because other factors – as yet unresolved – have since arisen to further confuse matters, such as the Government's professed wish to proceed with the privatisation of BR's freight business and their extremely contentious proposals for contraction of the coalmining industry (which is bound to have an adverse effect on BR).

Control Offices in York

As already mentioned in Chapter 2, the former Y&NM Board Room, located in the first floor of the old station buildings facing towards Tanner Row, is now a railway control office. From this commodious accommodation, George Hudson – 'The Railway King' – ruled his empire and held sway over lesser mortals, but now, from that same room, after some 150 years have elapsed, an organisation called 'Route Control' oversees the conduct of affairs and exercises its influence throughout the length and breadth of an empire far larger than anything that even Hudson could ever have imagined!

Railway control offices are very much a 20th century development. Some of the pre-Grouping railway companies experimented with various forms of control organisation in the days before World War 1 when the volume of freight traffic on offer was frequently so great as to almost cause embarrassment. Congestion and delay was rife, particularly around areas of heavy industry, and control offices emerged as a means of regulating freight and mineral traffic flows, avoidance of congestion, monitoring wagon supply arrangements, supervision of train performance and securing improved utilisation of resources. To this end, the NER introduced a freight traffic control organisation at Newport (Middlesbrough) in 1910, followed by a Tyneside Local Traffic Control at Newcastle in 1917, but the ultimate showpiece – indeed the NER's 'swan-song' – was the York Main Line Control located in Room 99 of the Main Headquarters building.

York Main Line Control

The Main Line Control, opened on 9 November 1922, just a couple of months before the Grouping, supervised 108 route miles of track between Shaftholme Junction (north of Doncaster) and Newcastle Central station. It was both a train and traffic control in that it exercised real-time supervision over main line train running and regulated the flows of freight traffic relative to the prevailing situation in the then busy marshalling yards at York, Darlington and around Tyneside, together with less important yards at Selby, Thirsk and Ferryhill. The most remarkable feature of the Main Line Control was its 'clockwork' diagram board.

The board was a 'running-time scale' diagrammatic representation of the controlled line, and it was fitted with a

Below:
York Main Line Control. Overall view of control board. *Railway Gazette*

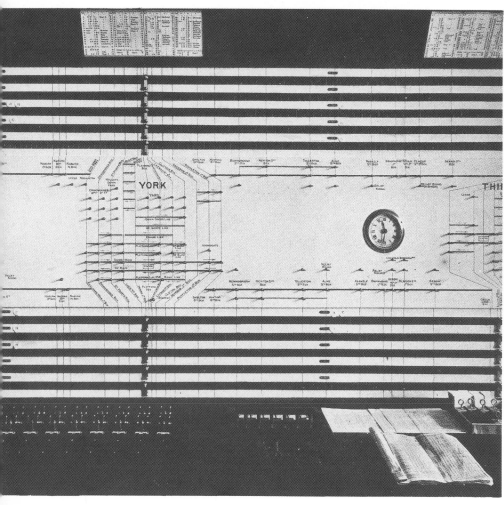

Above:
York Main Line Control. York detailed view. *Railway Gazette*

Below:
York Main Line Control. Northallerton/Thirsk detailed view. *Railway Gazette*

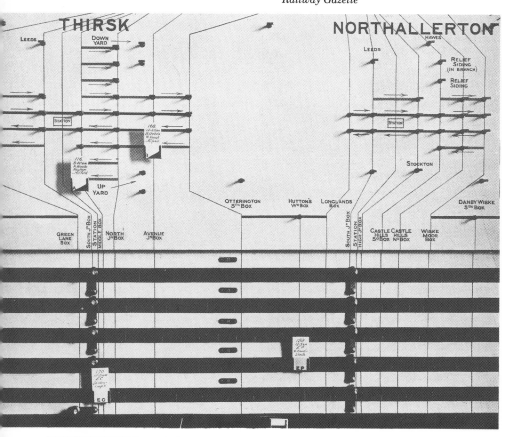

series of moving belts adjusted relative to the horizontal scale of the diagram to represent the average speed of trains in the various classes.

Actually there were five endless belts driven by clockwork mechanism (actuated by electric current) through variable pulleys at the top of the diagram board, which operated in the 'down' direction (ie, left to right). Similarly, five endless belts situated below the diagram board operated in the 'up' direction (ie, right to left). The endless belts (or 'cords' as they became known) moved continuously at five variable scale speeds, graded between 15 and 55 mph, and different coloured tickets to represent individual trains were hung on to a carrier to 'ride' on the belt nearest to the average speed for the class of train involved. The objective of this unique system was to enable control staff to see at a glance the *approximate* position of every train within the control area. The position of the carriers was adjusted by the train controllers as necessary to show the actual running of each train, according to information received from outside reporting points. As current reporting on telephone lines reserved exclusively for control purposes was an absolutely essential part of the system, the three train controllers who between them manipulated the diagram board on their shift of duty wore headsets, thus they were always available for instant communication with signalmen. (When a train was stationary for any reason, the ticket was taken off the cord and hung up on a peg; when the train concerned was reported as moving again the ticket was then returned to the cord.) The Traffic and Locomotive Controllers were seated behind the Train Controllers, and by observation of the diagram board they could readily work out their next moves without having to make enquiries of anyone else.

This somewhat unusual system, which at best could only be regarded as an approximate overview, or even as an 'aide-memoire', remained in being until 1940/41. Nonetheless, it was claimed that significant improvements in train regulation and performance – both passenger and freight – were achieved.

Another control office, York District, located at 37 Tanner Row, opened in 1937. (37 Tanner Row was once the 'North Eastern Hotel', purchased by the NER in 1899 and still used by BR as office accommodation.) In 1940, supervision of the main line south of Skelton Bridge was passed to York District Control, and in 1941 the moving belt system was abandoned when York District assumed control of the main line northwards to Northallerton. At the same time, control of the ECML between Northallerton and Newcastle was devolved to the then District Controls at Darlington, Sunderland and Newcastle. Both the Headquarters and York District Controls were 'evacuated' for the duration of World War 2 to bunkers burrowed into the embankment between the old station and the city walls (and these wartime emergency control bunkers still exist as storage for waste paper!).

After the cessation of hostilities, the Headquarters and York District Controls were transferred back to their original locations at Room 99 and 37 Tanner Row respectively, and, following the merger of the Eastern and North Eastern Regions of BR in 1967, a major reorganisation of control activities took place. Thus the Central Control (as the former Main Line Control had become known) was moved across from Room 99 to the erstwhile Y&NM Board Room to become 'Regional Control' for the enlarged Eastern Region. The new Regional Control office became effective on 13 April 1969. After the demise of Regions under 'Organising for Quality' a new title of 'Route Control' was adopted from 6 April 1992. Meanwhile, York District Control was closed on 3 October 1982, upon its function being overtaken by the then Divisional Control organisation at Leeds.

Route Control

The basic concept of 'control' has undergone radical changes since the first control offices were opened in the earlier years of this century. This is particularly noticeable in the case of freight traffic, where today's emphasis is very much focused upon disciplined block train load movement – operated under contracts tailored to meet the needs of individual customers – in sharp contrast to yesterday's mass movement of freight trains conveying individual wagon loads which frequently required shunting and resorting in a succession of marshalling yards. In other words, a high-volume bulk freight operation rather than attempting to carry everything to everywhere. Similarly, the degree of co-ordination formerly exercised between 'control' and a vast number of manually operated signal boxes has virtually disappeared due to the development of modern signalling, which means that one large power box (or IECC) can oversee large areas of railway comparable with the territory supervised by former control offices. Thus 'control' now exercises an overall monitoring function when things are running more or less to plan (according to the timetable), but it plays a prominent role in what might best be called 'incident management' (ie, to ensure that all incidents, mishaps, failures and other untoward occurrences are properly dealt with, emergency procedures followed through, train services adjusted, resources redeployed etc).

On the ECML, minute by minute control of all trains is first and foremost the responsibility of signalmen, either at large power boxes like King's Cross, Peterborough, Doncaster and Edinburgh, IECCs such as York and Tyneside, or smaller power boxes (which cover quite large areas) at Morpeth, Alnmouth and Tweedmouth to quote relevant examples. The former Divisional Controls have been replaced by Area Operations Centres (AOCs) – on the ECML these are located at King's Cross, Doncaster and Newcastle – but Route Control at York is the supreme body responsible for overseeing the running of the railway as a whole, irrespective of business 'ownership' throughout the geographical area of the erstwhile Eastern Region.

Whilst this work does not seek to delve too much into the whys and wherefores of control methods and procedures, a few words might be helpful in order to gain a broad appreciation of how Route Control affects the present day railway scene at York. The York Route Control – 'owned' by InterCity but it looks after the interests of *all* businesses! – has the final responsibility within its area of control for overseeing the correct conduct of all safety-related operational matters, coordination of all train services irrespective of business 'ownership', and overall incident management focused towards minimising the effect of mishaps/incidents on train services – and thereafter to ensure a speedy return to normal scheduled operation.

Some of the controllers within the office are designated as 'InterCity'. Others are 'Regional Railways' or 'Freight'; but the person in charge on each shift (formerly known as the Deputy Chief Controller – now Duty Operations Manager) holds authority to reconcile the (sometimes conflicting!) interests of the various businesses, in order to deal effectively with whatever emergency or out of the ordinary situation might arise.

Real-time monitoring within Route Control is achieved by TRUST (Train Running System TOPS), which is derived from TOPS (Total Operations Processing Systems) and linked to the ATR (Automatic Train Reporting) equipment allied to power box train describers. Thus it is possible to call up displays on VDU screens which depict the actual position of trains as they appear on the signalling control panels in major power boxes (or on the VDU screens at IECCs). TRUST represents a great advance upon the 'clockwork' train diagram board mentioned earlier.

Nevertheless, while many of the underlying principles still hold good, more sophisticated methods of achieving effective monitoring and control have evolved in recent years – thanks to computerised technology and modern communications/information systems.

The Future

Despite the variety of changes outlined in this chapter, some of which have swept away time-honoured and long established traditions, York is still very much in the forefront as a strategic railway centre.

What the future holds is anybody's guess! The proverbial 'crystal ball' has been obscured somewhat by privatisation, as set out in a Government White Paper (CM 2012) entitled 'New Opportunities for the Railways — The Privatisation of British Rail' presented to Parliament on 14 July 1992, and subsequently followed up by the 1993 Railways Bill. On Tuesday 2 February 1993, the Rt Hon John MacGregor MP, Secretary of State for Transport, announced in the House of Commons that InterCity's East Coast route was one of seven lines chosen to be franchised under the Government's privatisation timetable. 'Pilot Franchises' are expected to run for a year from April 1993 as self-contained BR subsidiaries before becoming private companies from Summer 1994, and who knows what happens next?

On the freight side the major problem still to be resolved at the time of going to print is the new contract between British Coal and the electricity generators which may or may not have an effect upon the coal traffic flows through York and the MGR activities at York Yard North. British Coal (another candidate for privatisation!) has more than enough problems of its own — compounded by the recession — but as long as coal from the north continues to be supplied to Aire Valley power stations then York must continue to play its part as a staging point for this traffic.

The other great unknown is, of course, the future of ABB at York where work looks like running out in 1994 unless drastic action is taken to redress the situation created by the uncertainties surrounding BR privatisation.

Nevertheless, it is not all doom and gloom for by 1995 York may well see daytime international services from Edinburgh to Paris and Brussels, assuming the Channel Tunnel opens as planned and if the proposed new trains are, in fact, ordered and built. Another welcome development is the new direct service to and from Manchester Airport scheduled for May 1993, and the outcome of the TransPennine electrification deliberations certainly is something awaited with much interest.

York's geographical situation as an important railway junction on InterCity's busy and profitable East Coast main line (despite the recession), also as the focal point of several well patronised Regional Railways passenger services, should ensure its pre-eminence well into the 21st century. Similarly, York's place in the railway hierarchy, as Headquarters centre for management and administration seems to be reasonably well assured — unless, of course, privatisation holds some unpleasant surprises which as yet cannot be foreseen. We must wait and see — but whatever the future has in store, York is and surely always will be a 'Rail Super Centre' of much interest and well worth a visit.

10. Preserving our Railway Heritage - The NRM Story

York is the home of the National Railway Museum (NRM), which made headlines when it was awarded the prestigious 'Museum of the Year Award' for 1991. (These annual awards are organised by National Heritage and sponsored by British Gas.) The announcement was made at a special lunchtime reception held at the Painters Hall, in London, on Tuesday 2 July 1991 when Dr John Coiley, then Head of the NRM, received the award during a presentation made by the Minister for the Arts – who at that time was the Rt Hon Timothy Renton. The Chairman of the Judges Committee, Sir Hugh Casson, said that the NRM had won the annual award for its outstanding 'Great Railway Show' housed in York's former goods station, which among other things, highlighted the social context of the age that made the railways.

Later the same day Dr Neil Cossons, Director of the National Museum of Science and Industry (of which the NRM is a part), made the long awaited announcement that the re-roofed 'Main Hall' – now called the 'Great Hall' – would reopen in the spring of 1992 thus doubling the area for display of the largest and most comprehensive collection of railway material in Europe. He went on to express a view that the NRM should be more than just an assembly of steam locomotives and other static exhibits: it must provide an insight into the modern railway system, and reflect the state-of-the-art technology currently being developed by a new generation of railway engineers. So why is the NRM located at York, and what is its history? To find the answer, one must go back to the early 1920s.

The 'Old' Railway Museum

In 1922, Sir Ralph Wedgwood – General Manager of the NER – initiated ideas to mark the centenary of the Stockton & Darlington Railway (which opened on 27 September 1825). Having decided that the event should be suitably cele-

brated, a procession of 'ancient' and 'modern' trains from Stockton to Darlington was organised (which actually took place on 2 July 1925), and the Railway Centenary celebrations were a huge success, being attended by Royalty and numerous official visitors from all over the world.

Concurrently with the development of the Railway Centenary plans, a meeting was convened by Mr Robert Bell – Assistant General Manager – who expressed the thought that 'whilst efforts had been made departmentally in the past to preserve interesting railway relics... there was a feeling that the time had arrived when some definite all-line scheme should be embarked upon'. Thus the first museum committee meeting was held on 29 March 1922, chaired by Mr Bell and attended by Mr J. B. Harper – Assistant General Superintendent – who for some years had taken a personal interest in preservation. Mr E. M. Bywell (Editor of

the NER Magazine) was appointed Secretary and Curator.

An inspection of the Queen Street workshops site soon followed, and it was agreed at the second meeting on 11 April 1922 that the old machine shop could be made suitable for large exhibits. A subsequent meeting held on 17 August 1922 reported 'work commenced'.

Initially, the LNER museum collection was only available for private visits by invited guests – such as VIPs from other railway administrations both at home and abroad. The exact date of the public opening is unclear and was not specifically recorded. However, from perusal of the first visitors book (courtesy of the

Below:
In this 1957 photograph, ex L&Y 'Pug' 0-4-0T No 51235 is manouvering the preserved NER 'Tennant' 2-4-0 at the old Railway Museum. *BR*

NRM archives), it was probably in January 1928 – judging from the names and addresses which appear therein.

Meanwhile the small exhibits previously stored in the Headquarters basement were placed on display in one of the rooms in the 'old' station from June 1928.

Up to the time of World War 2 in 1939, the LNER museum proved to be a popular attraction, and like many similar establishments it was closed 'for the duration'. As a matter of interest, it was reported at a meeting held on 19 August 1941 that the record-breaking preserved Great Western locomotive *City of Truro* had been moved away to a former small engine shed at Sprouston (on the Tweed-mouth-Kelso branch).

Similarly, some of the unique large exhibits were divided between the closed shed at Ferryhill (Co Durham) and the remote, though still at that time operational, ex-North British shed at Reedsmouth (on the Border Counties branch from Hexham). Most of the small exhibits were 'loaned' for safe keeping to the Bowes Museum at Barnard Castle. The 'old' museum was reopened following a brief ceremony held on 18 July 1947, and upon Nationalisation of the railways in 1948 it became the responsibility of the British Transport Commission (BTC). Subsequently, the small exhibits section in the 'old' station was modernised during 1958, but it was closed from 17 December 1966 and the display transferred to the main Queen Street building, which by that time had been reorganised and extended.

In 1951 the BTC established a Curator of Historical Records, and Mr. John Scholes, Curator of the successful Castle Museum in York, was appointed to this position, which he held until retirement in 1974. Plans were developed for a national transport museum, to be complemented by regional railway museums (of which York was already one), hence the early 1960s witnessed the opening of the Museum of British Transport in Clapham, the GWR Museum in Swindon and the Glasgow Transport Museum (the latter two were operated by the local authorities). Nonetheless, during the same period, the BTC, which operated the Museum of British Transport in Clapham (South London) was trying to rid itself of the burden of museum obligations. Eventually the 1968 Transport Act contained clauses transferring responsibility for railway relics to the Department of Education and Science (which at that time was the funding body for the Science Museum), which had no further accommodation available at their South Kensington premises. It became obvious, therefore, that a new building would be needed, and eventually, after much debate (which involved several contenders and really is a subject beyond the scope of this book), it emerged that York was the chosen site. The decision announced by Lord Eccles (then Paymaster General), on 10 May

Top:
The demise of Queen Street Museum in 1974, with NER No 910 being hauled out on temporary track. *K. Hoole Collection*

Above:
An interesting view of what is now the NRM 'Great Hall' turntable, taken on 21 December 1972 after BR had ceased to use the roundhouse. *BR*

1971, was doubtless swayed by considerations such as the availability of sites and buildings with rail access, the pre-eminence of York as both a railway and tourist centre in its own right plus the relative proximity to large concentrations of population with good rail and road communications.

On 31 December 1973, the 'old' railway museum closed its doors to the public for the last time, as preparations began to be made for a new era. The Museum of British Transport at Clapham had already closed on 23 April 1973.

The National Railway Museum (NRM)

The NRM concept arose from the 1968 Transport Act which, among other things, stipulated that the British Railways Board (BRB) would find and provide, in consultation with the Science Museum, a suitable site and building for the new museum. It was subsequently decided to refurbish and extend part of the York (North) MPD to rehouse most of the railway exhibits from the York Queen Street and Clapham museums and large amounts of material stored by the BRB. Work began in earnest on 16 January 1973. Nos 3 & 4 roundhouses were destined to become the 'Main Hall' of the new museum; No 3 shed dated from 1878 and it possessed a 60ft turntable, whereas No 4 shed was completed by 1915 and it had a 70ft turntable (replaced as recently as 1954).

Both sheds had been rebuilt and re-roofed by BR in 1957/58, and by 31 October 1974, work was sufficiently well

essarily all railway enthusiasts. Furthermore, under the terms of the 1968 Transport Act, the NRM has an inbuilt advantage because it has first claim upon redundant items (as relics) from BR without purchase cost, hence it is just possible to keep pace with change when in these days of rapid technological obsolescence relatively modern pieces of equipment, particularly signalling items, dating from the early 1950s are already almost 'vintage'!

On 1 March 1984, the Traction Maintenance Depot – in other words the modernised straight shed immediately adjacent to the then Main Hall – became available, so the NRM soon took it over and now it serves as a workshop for both maintenance and restoration purposes. Then on 1 April 1984, as a result of the 1983 National Heritage Act, the Science Museum (including its outstations such as the NRM) became a Trustee Museum instead of being run as a Government Department by the Office of Arts and Libraries. This reorganisation brought the Science Museum, of which the NRM is a part, in line with the other Trustee national museums. Shortly afterwards, but independently of the reorganisation, the Treasury agreed that, if the Trustees of a national museum wished to introduce charges, any monies resulting could be used for the benefit of the museum without penalty to the basic funding through the Grant-in-Aid. The Trustees of the Science Museum subsequently made the decision to introduce admission charges at the NRM from 6 April 1987 so that the resulting funds would be available to develop and improve the museum. Without extra funds the museum would be unable to respond adequately to the challenge of providing a modern technical museum. Not unnaturally, this resulted in customer resistance and for a while a significant drop in attendances became evident. Nonetheless, it can safely be said that the NRM is now as popular as ever: indeed, it has become an absolute 'must' to the thousands of overseas visitors who come to York each year, not forgetting the numerous school parties on educational visits.

Since it opened in 1975, the NRM has

advanced to enable the Main Hall to be handed over to the NRM so that a start could be made to assemble and install the exhibits. By skilful design the BR architects succeeded in retaining some of the 'atmosphere' of the former steam sheds in the new Main Hall, while at the same time conveying a light and spacious impression. Apart from the building and construction work, major operations were mounted, in conjunction with BR, to transfer the large exhibits from both the Queen Street and Clapham museums and other storage sites. The target date for the opening of the NRM was, most appropriately, 27 September 1975 in order to coincide with the 150th anniversary of the Stockton & Darlington Railway, and on the day the carefully laid plans duly came to fruition. HRH Prince Philip, Duke of Edinburgh, did the honours and the NRM had well and truly arrived in York.

Much of the credit for organising and overseeing the progress of the NRM project without doubt belongs to Dr John Coiley (whose appointment as 'Keeper'

had been announced on 11 July 1974) and to Mr Peter Semmens, his Assistant Keeper. The new museum was a great success right from the start, though it has to be said that admission was free in those days. Nevertheless, in the first year since opening just over 2 million visitors passed through its doors, and by the time the 10th anniversary was reached in 1985, the cumulative total had reached nearly 13 million. The public had definitely voted with their feet, and most of the committed railway enthusiast fraternity, some of whom had been distinctly unhappy about the demise of the old museums and apprehensive about the new one, appeared to be well satisfied with the result.

The principal objective of the NRM can perhaps best be stated as being one of continually aiming to be a 'living' museum – rather than a 'dead' one. Its job goes far beyond preservation, exhibition and restoration: it is to interpret both the past and the present railway scene for the benefit (and education) of the majority of visitors, who are not nec-

had one main problem with its York site: the public exhibition area focussed on the Main Hall was just not big enough. In fact, one could almost be tempted to say that within the space of a few years the NRM had become a victim of its own success. Despite some of the National Collection being on display elsewhere, such as at Swindon and in the Science Museum in South Kensington, there was a sizeable 'reserve collection' at York not available for viewing by the public. In 1976, the NRM acquired the former York goods station and associated office block (the Peter Allen building) which were soon filled with items in store.

For some years the NRM endeavoured to find ways and means to develop a much larger display area, and a lot of detailed planning was undertaken. A report prepared in 1987 had recommended radical changes, and on 3 July 1988 (during celebrations to mark the 50th anniversary of *Mallard* attaining a world speed record for steam of 126 mph), Dr Neil Cossons announced long term development plans intended to double the display space and – 'to provide Britain – the birthplace of the public railway – with the largest and most comprehensive railway museum in the world'. Excellent news indeed! But, as always, the problem was money – or rather the lack of it – which precluded positive steps from being taken until adequate funds were forthcoming. As discussions with the Office of Arts & Libraries and the Treasury about funding the project were likely to be protracted, it was fairly obvious that a realistic start date seemed rather remote.

The Re-roofing Saga

It had been known for some years that the concrete beams of the roof of the Main Hall were failing, and the proposed development plans actually included an element of financial provision for replacement. These concrete beams, which formed the roof structure, were cast from a high-chloride content cement widely used during the 1950s and valued for its quick-drying properties. Unfortunately, however, it is now known that, especially in the presence of moisture, the chlorides accelerate rusting of the reinforcing rods in the beams which leads to eventual structural failure. Once it was established by the structural engineers that work to renew the roof **must** start in April 1990, all forward planning, of sheer necessity, took on a new and particular urgency. The pressing need to do something about the roof proved to be the turning point. What could have been a disastrous situation, involving the closure of the Main Hall for at least a year – and probably even longer – was seized upon as an opportunity. Here was the chance to at least start the planned development of the museum site: the roof problem concentrated everyone's minds, and arising therefrom was born the concept of what

was to become 'The Great Railway Show'.

The onerous task of planning and co-ordinating the £6.5 million project fell to the newly appointed Deputy Keeper, Rob Shorland-Ball, who took up his post on 5 October 1987 following the retirement of Peter Semmens on 11 September 1987. As the Main Hall was the principal display area of the museum, it was apparent that major roof work, priceless objects and visitors could not co-exist. Obviously, with the Main Hall being out of commission for a long time, it was absolutely unthinkable to close for the duration of the work so this had to be avoided by maximising use of the museum's other resources – in other words, the Peter Allen building. Not only was the Peter Allen building the obvious and only alternative main display area, but it had the potential to remain in use as extra space once the Main Hall reopened. Two fundamental decisions were soon to be made to the effect that there must be no decline in standards, and, both in the interim stage and after the re-roofing was finished, the NRM's presentation should be more in line with the expectations of the increasingly heritage-conscious British public.

The creation of the 'Great Railway Show' underlined the need to provide a dedicated crossing of the adjacent Leeman Road, a busy thoroughfare, for visitors and in this respect the local planning authority – York City Council – recommended a subway as the only ideal solution. Another vital element to be resolved was the storage of items not in the 'Great Railway Show' but displaced from the Main Hall. The cost of commercial storage for huge items like railway locomotives was enormous, so the idea of the 'NRM on Tour' was developed. The location proved to be Swindon, thanks to Tarmac Properties Ltd, who are working towards the establishment of a Heritage Centre at the former Swindon Works site. By April 1990 'The NRM on Tour' had assembled an impressive collection of large exhibits at Swindon, including the famous *Mallard,* and in fact during 1990 more of the National Collection was on display than previously had been the case.

The NRM in its original form closed on 28 February 1990, and the 'Great Railway Show' duly opened on the following day, 1 March 1990. Re-roofing work started on 1 April 1990, then following removal of the defective structure, together with its forest of supporting columns, construction of the new roof – of a radically different design – was soon under way. The opportunity to create a lofty structure with a single-span covering an area almost as wide as the concourse at London's St Pancras station – that reduced the admission of natural light, was relatively maintenance free, completely insulated, left an uncluttered floor area and greatly enhanced the ambience within the building – was irre-

sistable. As the new roof took shape, the absence of numerous supporting pillars was quickly seen to advantage and soon the overall impression of internal spaciousness and light became apparent. Alterations were also made to the track layout within the hall, and the smaller of the two turntables was removed so as to provide parallel lines for display of carriages and other rolling stock. Actually, quite a lot of heart-searching went on concerning this particular aspect, and to quote Rob Shorland-Ball: 'There was never any doubt that the most dramatic, effective and appropriate way to display a large collection of steam locomotives was round a turntable. The display of rolling stock, and, particularly, long carriages, around the second turntable was arguably less successful. Carriages were not usually stored in that way on the working railway; they presented a rather unattractive array of carriage ends to the viewer on the turntable; the tapered spaces in between the radial tracks were awkward to use for small objects; and the short track lengths throughout the hall meant that trains – or even two-car multiple-units – were almost impossible to accommodate.' A conclusion with which, upon reflection, one must feel bound to agree.

The 'New' NRM

The 'Great Railway Show', located within the original goods station, was first planned as an interim measure designed to maintain a public 'presence' and keep the NRM 'alive' while the Main Hall was closed for re-roofing and refurbishment. Fortunately, events proved the 'Great Railway Show' to be such a success that a decision was soon taken to continue the exhibition on a permanent basis. The 'Great Railway Show' – now restyled as 'Travelling by Train for Goods and People' – while somewhat enhanced remains largely unchanged, and the former goods station warehouse premises are collectively known as the 'South Hall'.

In effect, the new NRM now presents two faces to its visitors. The Great Hall (so-called after the Great Hall at the old Euston station), tells the story of the technology of railways – past, present and future – whereas the South Hall conveys an underlying theme which reflects upon the experience of travelling by train from the early beginnings of railways up to the present day.

Almost as if by coincidence, the new era signalled a change in the NRM's top management. Dr John Coiley retired and the appointment of his successor, Mr Andrew Dow, took effect from 6 January 1992. To a significant degree the development of the NRM since its inception has been in the hands of Dr Coiley, and, without doubt, his successor has inherited a living vibrant museum. Mr Dow, son of the famous historian the late George Dow whose many contributions to railway literature have come to

Above:
A recent view of the NRM 'South Hall' interior – showing the former 'Great Railway Show' – which is housed in the ex-Leeman Road main warehouse. *Crown Copyright; NRM, York*

Above right:
A very up to date impression of the NRM 'Great Hall' with a new 'Networker' unit on exhibition framed by a complete ring section of the Channel Tunnel. Note '9F' *Evening Star* **in the background.** *Crown Copyright; NRM, York*

be regarded as authoritative works of reference, combines senior management and business experience with a keen interest in railways and is therefore well placed to ensure the continuing success of the new NRM. Already, Mr Dow has restated the principles which John Coiley and Rob Shorland-Ball had evolved about the museum's purpose; he believes it is important to recognise the nature of the visiting public of whom dedicated railway enthusiasts are really a minority compared with the families and tourists who comprise the majority. For this reason, it is his view that the emphasis upon steam for its own sake

must be kept in perspective, hence more prominence needs to be given to diesel traction, electrification and the modern scene, in order to stimulate and retain continued interest. In the final analysis, it is all about the maintenance of a sensible 'balance' – in this respect the new NRM has done very well.

Additionally, it must be mentioned that the NRM offers excellent facilities to researchers of railway history, supported by a comprehensive collection of archive photographs in the museum's Reference Library: the library is open free to researchers every weekday (except Saturdays). Also, the NRM pro-

vides a popular facility to organised school parties, which helps considerably to secure a place for railways – in a number of subjects – within the framework of the National Curriculum.

The climax of all the planning and hard work put into the new NRM project came on Wednesday 15 April 1992 when the Great Hall was opened to public viewing. Then followed the formal opening performed by HRH The Duke of Kent on Thursday 16 April, and up to the time of writing in July 1992 a generally favourable response has been forthcoming from both visitors and the press.

In a word, it is excellent.

Friends of the NRM

As in the case of numerous national and local institutions, hospitals and the like, the NRM has its 'Friends'. The Friends of the National Railway Museum (FNRM), a Registered Charity No 273829, celebrated its 10th birthday on 16 May 1987 and its stated objectives are 'Encouragement, fostering, assistance and promotion in any manner of the work and activities of the NRM including work and activity carried out jointly or in co-operation with the Science Museum or any other Museum, art gallery, preservation society or similar organisation'. In practice, this is taken to mean the provision of encouragement, and resources, for activities which the NRM itself may be unable to undertake for whatever reason. The jewel in the crown must be the restored Stanier Pacific No 46229 *Duchess of Hamilton,* and another of the Friends' many positive achievements was the restoration to running order of the 'A4' No 4468 *Mallard.*

Membership of the 'Friends' carries with it a number of privileges such as unlimited free admission to the NRM during normal visiting hours, an excellent quarterly newsletter, priority bookings on FNRM railtours and invitations to meetings, together with information about events connected with the museum.

Finally, of course, there is always the personal sense of satisfaction in belonging to a group of like-minded people committed to the future success of the NRM.

Left:
The NRM Great Hall's ambience is demonstrated in this overview. Note the statue of George Stephenson which came from the other 'Great Hall' at the old Euston station in London. *Crown Copyright; NRM, York*

Top right:
Exterior view of the NRM Great Hall showing the new roof. The GN 'somersault' signal can just be glimpsed centre left of picture. *Crown Copyright; NRM, York*

Right:
Up to date plan of the new NRM internal layout. *NRM, York / Peter Leonard & Co*

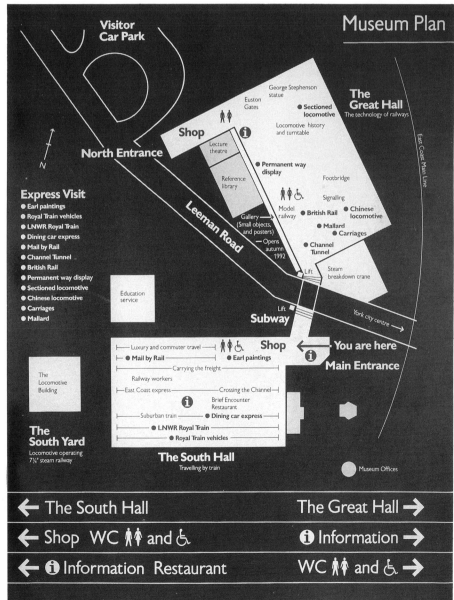

11. York's 'Other Railway' – The Derwent Valley

The Derwent Valley Light Railway (DVLR), which opened in 1913 to convey passengers and freight between York (Layerthorpe) and Cliff Common (for Selby), and which lost its regular passenger service as long ago as 1926, was remarkable in that it survived two world wars, the Grouping, Nationalisation and a variety of other crises. In its latter days it even embarked upon a steam hauled passenger service, aimed at the tourist market, during the summer months – unfortunately without much success – though right up to the mid-1970s it carried quite respectable tonnages of freight traffic.

Like many other light railways – though it managed to survive longer than most – the DVLR had its origins under the provisions of the Light Railways Act of 1896. The agricultural depression in the 1890s assisted the passage of this particular Act, making it possible for local lines, either of standard or narrow gauge, to be built to help farmers to get their produce to towns and markets more cheaply. The Act not only relaxed some of the physical requirements of a full scale railway, in respect of such things as track, signalling, level crossings, fencing and other mandatory standards, but it also enabled lines to be authorised by Order of the Light Railway Commissioners without the costly procedure of an Act of Parliament.

Subsequently, a joint committee was formed composed of the Riccall and Escrick Rural District Councils, together with prominent local landowners, and following numerous delays (mainly concerned with raising the necessary capital) work on constructing the line commenced at the Cliff Common end in 1911, although the DVLR Co as such had been formed in 1907. On 29 October 1912, the Wheldrake-Cliff Common section was opened for freight traffic with-

Right:
Map of Derwent Valley Light Railway (1913). *R. D. Pulleyn Collection*

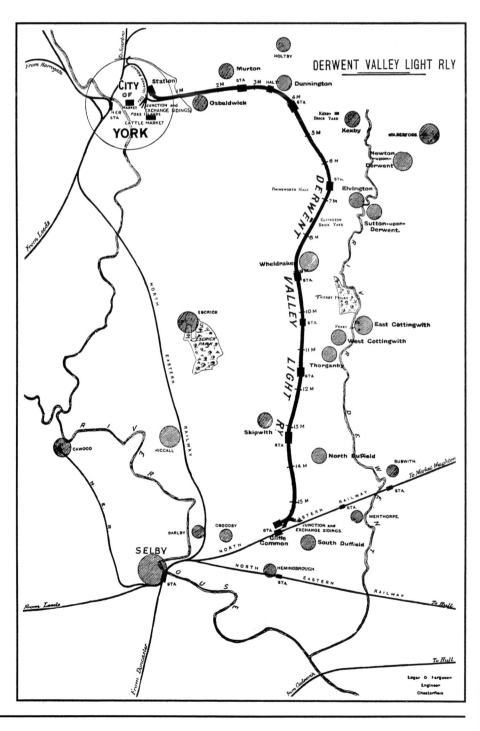

out any formality. Then on Saturday 19 July 1913, the line was opened throughout with due ceremony. Lady Deramore, (wife of the Chairman) 'cut the ribbon' at York Layerthorpe station to set off the inaugural passenger train – which was hauled by NER locomotive No 1679 (Class 190 2-2-4T) borrowed for the occasion and suitably adorned.

Regular public services started to run on Monday 21 July 1913, comprising initially three weekday trains each way between York (Layerthorpe) and Cliff Common, plus an additional York-Wheldrake service. The original passenger stock consisted of two ex-NER coaches painted in dark blue with gold lettering, first and third class accommodation being provided. The journey time for the 16 miles between York and Cliff Common was scheduled to take 50/58min but as 'mixed' trains were frequently operated – which involved attaching/detaching wagons at stations enroute – punctuality cannot have been too reliable. When the line opened, an agreement was entered into with the NER who undertook to provide a steam locomotive at an inclusive figure per annum including driver, fireman and stores. Later, only the locomotive was hired, the DVLR employing its own footplate crew and providing its own stores. In 1925, the DVLR purchased a 100hp Sentinel locomotive – the first of its kind to be tried out on a British railway. Whilst the Sentinel was quite a capable machine, particularly for shunting duties, it was not really up to DVLR 'main line' work and eventually it was sold to a firm in Darlington for use in their private siding.

Meanwhile, in an attempt to reduce the cost of operating the passenger service, a back-to-back Ford rail-bus unit was purchased. Even though running costs were reputedly reduced to something like 5d per mile, compared with 1s 5d per mile for steam operation, the decline in business could not be arrested following the growth of country bus services during the early 1920s, and regular passenger trains ran for the last time on 31 August 1926.

Special excursion trains ran occasionally up to 1939, though from 1954 onwards the line was visited by a few railway enthusiasts' specials organised by various societies. (After the cessation of passenger services the two rail-bus units finished their days on the County Donegal narrow gauge system in Ireland following adaptation to run on 3ft gauge tracks.)

Construction of the line did not present much in the way of engineering difficulties, the surrounding terrain being generally flat, and the original track was bought second hand from the Midland Railway – said to have come from the Settle-Carlisle line. The northern terminal of the line was at York (Layerthorpe), where a junction was effected with the NER Foss Islands branch adjacent to Hallfield Road bridge. Layerthorpe pos-

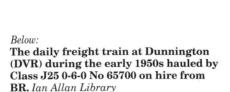

Right:
The Derwent Valley's one and only signal! This diminutive specimen was to be found on the York side of Wheldrake station, and the signal wire was connected with the level crossing gates so that the arm would only move to the 'off' position when the gates were closed against road traffic. *R. D. Pulleyn*

Below:
The daily freight train at Dunnington (DVR) during the early 1950s hauled by Class J25 0-6-0 No 65700 on hire from BR. *Ian Allan Library*

sessed a sizeable yard, and the passenger station had one long single platform. The various tracks converged into a single line east of Layerthorpe yard and the DVLR 'main line' proceeded via Osbaldwick, Murton, Dunnington, Elvington and Wheldrake on its way to join the NER Selby-Market Weighton-Driffield line in a group of exchange sidings at Cliff Common. The total distance of running line was just over 16 miles.

No signalling equipment was required under the terms of the Light Railway Order as the line was worked under the 'one engine in steam' principle ('One Train Working' in present day jargon). The various ground frames at the intermediate stations, together with running line connections at Layerthorpe and Cliff Common, were locked by 'Annetts Key' (which was carried by the train driver as his sole authority to occupy the single line). The DVLR did, however, possess one solitary signal which was at Wheldrake, where a sharp bend from the Elvington direction obscured the driver's view of the level crossing gates. Strangely enough, this signal had a notch cut in the arm to make it look like a distant; actually, the arm was connected over a pulley direct to the near-side crossing gate, thus it was 'pulled off' by the

manual operation of closing the gate to road traffic! (This unusual signal was made in the joiners shop of the long-gone Sand Hutton light railway which, in its day, connected with the NER York-Market Weighton line at Warthill.)

The DVLR enjoyed modest fortunes in the years between the two world wars, but following the outbreak of World War 2 in 1939 the line really came into its own as vast quantities of freight traffic were encountered. Much of the track was covered in weeds due to deferred maintenance and legend has it that the War Office ordered that no weeding should be done so that the DVLR could retain its natural camouflage. (Apparently, RAF aerial photographs gave no indication of the DVLR's presence!) In addition to government traffic for adjacent airfields etc, agricultural traffic increased spectacularly due to wartime restrictions on road transport brought about by fuel rationing.

Not unexpectedly, freight traffic declined in the years following the end of World War 2, and gradually the emphasis shifted towards concentration on a smaller range of bulk commodities. For instance, a mechanised coal concentration depot was set up on DVLR territory at Layerthorpe yard. This depot was

opened on 12 October 1964 (it does not exist today). A ready-mixed concrete depot was established in the station yard at Osbaldwick in 1959, and enlarged in 1965 to deal with full train loads in 'Presflo' wagons. Then, at Dunnington, a grain drying plant was built on land (originally owned by the DVLR and sold to the firm who developed the site), which soon became private siding connected. Barley for various distillers in Scotland was despatched in bulk grain wagons for many years, though latterly owners' tank wagons were used for this traffic.

By the mid-1960s, freight traffic on the southern end of the DVLR had dwindled away, and when in the so-called 'Beeching' era BR decided to close their Selby-Market Weighton-Driffield branch in 1965, the DVLR was isolated at Cliff Common. This left the DVLR with no option but to close the southern extremity of their line, and an Abandonment Order was made on 9 February 1965. The last passenger trains to traverse the

Wheldrake-Cliff Common section were two RCTS enthusiasts specials which ran on Saturdays 9 and 16 January 1965, and the last freight trip ran on 22 February 1965. Subsequently, the Wheldrake-Elvington section was closed from 19 June 1968 (the last freight trip ran on 17 May 1968), followed by the Elvington-Dunnington closure from 19 January 1973 (the last freight trip ran on 22 June 1972).

Interestingly, the word 'Light' was formally omitted from the Company's title from 23 March 1973 and henceforth the railway became known as the 'Derwent Valley' (DVR).

With the advent of dieselisation on BR and the resultant demise of steam, it was decided in 1961 to hire a 204hp diesel-mechanical shunting locomotive from BR, which in the event proved to be very economical. This prompted a decision in 1969 to purchase from BR a couple of Drewry 0-6-0 diesel shunters, originally BR Nos D2298 and D2245 of Class 04, which became DVR Nos 1 and 2 respectively (No 1 was subsequently named *Lord Wenlock* after the first Chairman of the DVLR).

The opening of the NRM at York in 1975 and the increasing popularity of York as a tourist centre caused the DVR directors to consider the possibility of introducing a 'vintage steam' type of ser-

vice as an attraction for tourists, railway enthusiasts, school parties and even the general public. It was thought that the DVR possessed potential for such a venture by virtue of it being the nearest independent railway to the NRM, and in any case the track was being strengthened around that time to bring it up to standard for modern heavy axle-weight freight vehicles. In the event, these improvements proved to be acceptable to the Railways Inspectorate for the introduction of a vintage steam service.

Accordingly, by arrangement with the NRM, an initial trial run was made between Layerthorpe and Dunnington on 16 September 1976, utilising the ex-LNWR 2-4-0 locomotive *Hardwicke* hauling the Duke of Sutherland's former personal saloon. This test run worked

successfully, so in the following month the DVR ran three publicly advertised market testing trips in one day, again using *Hardwicke* but this time with three coaches hired from BR.

Despite bad weather, some 350 passengers were carried during that day (Saturday 9 October 1976), and a decision was made to run a once daily service (Mondays excepted) between May and October 1977. The inaugural journey on

Below:
The Derwent Valley's total locomotive stock, Nos 1 & 2, on 9 October 1976. Both locomotives were purchased from BR; prior to withdrawal from service they were Nos D2298 and D2245 respectively (of Class 04). *Ian Allan Library*

4 May 1977 was honoured by the presence of York's Lord Mayor, a reminder of the original opening of the line in 1913 when the then Lord Mayor participated, and things went well that summer – despite generally poor holiday weather, with some 10,000 passengers being carried. It was decided, therefore, to repeat the experiment – with slight modifications – for summer 1978, but the results were not as encouraging as in the previous year. Whether or not the novelty had worn off by the time summer 1979 came around is debatable, but the promise shown in 1977 failed to materialise, notwithstanding the offer of a free bus service from the NRM to Layerthorpe station to connect with the afternoon steam train.

The fares charged seemed to be quite reasonable (£1 return for adults and 50p for children), and for a modest 50p supplement one could travel first class. After due consideration, the DVR decided it could not continue with this venture and the advertised steam workings ceased on 31 August 1979 – though pre-arranged party bookings were honoured until November.

The rolling stock used for the steam service was the 0-6-0T *Joem* and three corridor bogie coaches purchased from BR (repainted in the original DVLR livery of dark blue, lined, lettered and numbered in gold). *Joem* was formerly a Class J72 locomotive No 69023 built by BR at Darlington North Road Works in

1951 to an ex-NER design originated by Wilson Worsdell as long ago as 1898. It may be recalled that *Joem* was at one time on the Keighley and Worth Valley Railway. Following the end of the vintage steam service after the 1979 season, the coaches were sold, and *Joem* now belongs to the North Eastern Locomotive Preservation Group, and, it is pleasing to know, is still in working order.

During the early 1970s, freight traffic on the DVR was still fairly buoyant. For example, in the year 1971, 36,980 tons of coal and coke, 5,317 tons of cement, 11,461 tons of oil, 9,879 tons of grain, 5,734 tons of sugar beet and smaller quantities of fertiliser and scrap were carried, and at that time the Chairman – Mr Roy Cook – expressed optimism as to

Left:
A May 1977 picture of *Joem* waiting to depart from York Layerthorpe station (DVR) bound for Dunnington.
R. Wildsmith

Below left:
York Layerthorpe (DVR) engine shed, which was situated at the platform end with *Joem* inside after an afternoon passenger train working to Dunnington and back on 10 August 1979. *M. Dunnett*

Below:
***Joem* heads a mixed train towards Dunnington on 6 May 1977.** *R. Wildsmith*

the line's future. Mr Cook's own company, Yorkshire Grain Driers at Dunnington, had expanded and thrived as large quantities of malting barley were despatched by rail to whisky distilleries in Scotland.

Nevertheless, by the end of the decade, things had changed for the worse. The decline in the domestic coal market resulted in the coal concentration depot at Layerthorpe being closed, and the volume of malting barley was depressed by falling whisky sales. On the other hand, a fuel oil depot had been established on DVR territory at Layerthorpe, but the line as a whole had by then become uneconomical to operate. In the final analysis, it was decided to close the line betwen Layerthorpe and Dunnington, and the last train ran on Sunday 27 September 1981. This was an enthusiasts special – organised in conjunction with the BR Staff Railway Society – hauled by diesel locomotive No 1 *Lord Wenlock* and composed of coaches hired from BR. All that remained thereafter was a few yards of track at Layerthorpe itself in order to enable BR to serve the fuel oil depot until the contract finally terminated in October 1988. Thus the DVR passed into oblivion, as indeed has BR's Foss Islands branch, and a formal notice was lodged in 1990 (under Section 83 of the 1962 Transport Act) seeking to abandon the final portion of the line at Layerthorpe leading up to the point of

connection with BR at Hallfield Road bridge.

Traces of the DVR are already beginning to vanish and a recent survey revealed that the Layerthorpe station site has been cleared altogether, though the yard area has been converted into an industrial estate. Similarly, the sites of the former stations at Osbaldwick, Dunnington and Elvington have been developed for industrial purposes, and no trace now remains of the DVR at these three locations. Nature has reclaimed the site of where the erstwhile DVLR/NER exchange sidings used to be at Cliff Common, and there is nothing to be seen of the former station at Cottingwith. However, three of the distinctive DVLR style of stations still survive at Wheldrake, Thorganby and Skipwith – the former two examples now being in a semi-derelict condition, whereas the latter has been converted into a private dwelling. Finally, although the station and yard site at Murton is now virtually unrecognisable, having been incorporated into the premises of a scrap metal processing firm, nearby there still remains a few yards of DVR track adjacent to 'Murton Park' where the Yorkshire Museum of Farming is located. Here also is the base of the Great Yorkshire Railway Preservation Society which came to Murton recently, having been obliged to vacate their former location at Starbeck near Harrogate.

Appendices

Appendix 1
Local stations around York – Closure Dates

Station	Passenger closure date	Freight closure date
Alne	5 May 1958	10 Aug 1964
Balne	15 Sep 1958	6 Jul 1964
Beningbrough	15 Sep 1958	5 Jul 1965
(Renamed from Shipton 1898)		
Bolton Percy	13 Sep 1965	27 Apr 1964
Brompton	6 Sep 1965	6 Sep 1965
Cattal	Still open	3 May 1965
Cawood	1 Jan 1930	2 May 1960
Church Fenton	Still open	3 Oct 1966
Cliff Common	20 Sep 1954	27 Jan 1964
(Line Selby-Driffield closed 12 June1965)		
Copmanthorpe	5 Jan 1959	4 May 1964
Earswick	29 Nov 1965	7 June 1965
(Renamed from Huntington 1874; The 'Flag and Whistle' public house now occupies the site of Earswick station)		
Easingwold	29 Nov 1948	27 Dec 1957
Escrick	8 June 1953	11 Sep 1961
Fangfoss	5 Jan 1959	7 June 1965
Goldsborough	15 Sep 1958	3 May 1965
Hambleton	14 Sep 1959	7 Sep 1964
Hammerton	Still open	3 May 1965
Haxby	22 Sep 1930	10 Aug 1964
Heck	15 Sep 1958	29 Apr 1963
Hessay	15 Sep 1958	4 May 1964
(Hessay temporarily closed 20 Sep 1915-12 July 1920)		
Holtby	11 Sep 1939	1 Jan 1951
(Renamed from Gate Helmsley 1872)		
Hopperton	15 Sep 1958	5 Nov 1962
(Renamed from Allerton 1925)		
Knaresborough	Still open	3 May 1965
Marston Moor	15 Sep 1958	3 May 1965
Moss	8 June 1953	8 June 1953
Naburn	8 June 1953	6 July 1964
Otterington	15 Sep 1958	10 Aug 1964
Pilmoor	5 May 1958	14 Sep 1959
Pocklington	29 Nov 1965	29 Nov 1965
(Station buildings now used by Pocklington School as a sports centre)		
Poppleton	Still open	4 May 1964
Raskelf	5 May 1958	10 Aug 1964
Riccall	15 Sep 1958	6 July 1964
Sessay	15 Sep 1958	10 Aug 1964
Sherburn in Elmet	13 Sep 1965	1 May 1967
(Sherburn in Elmet reopened 9 July 1984)		
Stamford Bridge	29 Nov 1965	29 Nov 1965
Strensall	22 Nov 1930	10 Aug 1964
(Strensall Halt, at Strensall No 2 Crossing, opened in March 1926 and closed 22 Nov 1930)		
Templehirst	6 Mar 1961	6 July 1964
Thirsk	Still open	3 Oct 1966
(The goods station was at Thirsk Town, the original terminus of the Leeds & Thirsk Railway)		
Tollerton	1 Nov 1965	6 Sep 1965
Ulleskelf	Still open	27 Apr 1964
Warthill	5 Jan 1959	7 June 1965
(Renamed from Stockton on the Forest 1896)		
Wistow	1 Jan 1930	2 May 1960
York Leeman Road	–	3 Jan 1972
York Foss Islands	–	6 Aug 1984

Appendix 2
York MPD summary of allocated 'Deltic' locomotives

1. 15 Deltics were transferred to York during May 1979 viz:
   55002/04/05/06/08/09/10/11/13/14/16/17/19/21/22.
2. Another four Deltics were transferred to York during June 1981:
   55007/12/15/18.
3. The remaining three Deltics out of a fleet total of 22 did not transfer to York and
   were withdrawn from traffic:
   55001 – 06.01.80/003 – 31.12.80/020 – 06.01.80.
4. The 19 Deltics allocated to York were withdrawn from traffic:
   55005/06 – 08.02.81; 55012 – 18.05.81
   55018 – 12.10.81; 55004 – 01.11.81
   55011 – 08.11.81; 55014 – 22.11.81
   55013 – 20.12.81; 55010 – 24.12.81
   55016 – 30.12.81; 55007/08/17/19/21 – 31.12.81
   55002/09//15/22 – 02.01.82
5. The following 7 Deltics have been preserved:
   55002 (9002) *KOYLI*
   55009 (9009) *Alycidon*
   55015 (9015) *Tulyar*
   55016 (9016) *Gordon Highlander*
   55019 (9019) *Royal Highlander*
   55022 (9000) *Royal Scots Greys Fusilier*
   Additionally, the prototype Deltic has been preserved.

Notes:
The Prototype Deltic's entry into service was in October 1955, when it was based at
Liverpool. Transferred to Eastern Region in January 1959. Returned to Vulcan
Foundry in March 1961, thence to the Science Museum in April 1963.

Deltic No 55015 was present at the Rainhill events on 24/25/26 May 1980.

The last Deltic trip under BR auspices was No 55015 on a King's Cross-Edinburgh
special train on Saturday 2 January 1982. Worked by No 55022 on a return journey,
with No 55009 being on standby at Newcastle.

Appendix 3
Locomotive Allocations

Unfortunately, official engine allocation lists have survived only from December
1923, but because of York's popularity with early railway photographers we have a
photographic record of many of the old engines. Even so some of the smaller
engines have gone unphotographed due, no doubt, to the photographers' desire to
capture something new from Darlington or Gateshead rather than photograph an
old locomotive which had been around for many years.

York Locomotive Allocation 6 December 1923

LNER Class	NER Class			
A7	Y	4-6-2T	(2)	1113, 1192
B15	S2	4-6-0	(7)	799, 813, 817, 820, 821, 822, 823 (Note 1)
B16	S3	4-6-0	(28)	844, 845, 847, 848, 849, 908, 911, 921, 923, 925, 927, 933, 936, 942, 1371, 1374, 1377, 2364, 2366, 2368, 2370, 2372, 2373, 2374, 2376, 2378, 2380, 2382 (Note 2)
C6	V V/09	4-4-2	(4)	698, 699, 702, 1792
C7	Z	4-4-2	(15)	717, 721, 2163, 2164, 2165, 2166, 2167, 2168, 2169, 2171, 2172, 2198, 2199, 2202, 2208
D20	R	4-4-0	(15)	707, 708, 711, 713, 724, 1026, 1260, 1672, 2018, 2021, 2022, 2027, 2028, 2101, 2104
D21	R1	4-4-0	(7)	1237, 1238, 1239, 1240, 1241, 1245, 1246
–	901	2-4-0	(1)	910
–	1440	2-4-0	(1)	486

G6	BTP	0-4-4T	(3)	255, 466, 951
–	398	0-6-0	(3)	392, 1164, 1412
J21	C	0-6-0	(8)	34, 534, 807, 1516, 1803, 1804, 1807, 1809
J24	P	0-6-0	(1)	1844
J26	P2	0-6-0	(11)	412, 442, 525, 554, 818, 831, 1098, 1130, 1200, 1366, 1674
J27	P3	0-6-0	(5)	2342, 2343, 2354, 2355, 2383
J71	E	0-6-0T	(11)	237, 399, 447, 1084, 1085, 1134, 1140, 1163, 1167, 1758, 1831
J72	E1	0-6-0T	(9)	1746, 2307, 2309, 2313, 2328, 2331, 2332, 2333, 2334
J77	290	0-6-0T	(6)	138, 999, 1000, 1346, 1348, 1431 (Note 2)
X3	190	2-2-4T	(1)	1679

*Ex-GN engines outstationed at York
(1924 numbers)*

C1	–	4-4-2	(2)	4424, 4447
D2	–	4-4-0	(8)	4180, 4331, 4386, 4387, 4390, 4396, 4398 (and one not identified)
D3	–	4-4-0	(2)	4071, 4348

Total 150

Notes:
1 One unidentified engine of this class outstationed at Scarborough.
2 One unidentified engine of this class outstationed at Normanton.

York Locomotive Allocation 31 December 1932

A7	4-6-2T	(3)	1113, 1174, 1193
B13	4-6-0	(1)	775
B15	4-6-0	(8)	787, 797, 799, 813, 817, 820, 821, 822
B16	4-6-0	(19)	844, 847, 908, 923, 926, 927, 1373, 1377, 2364, 2366, 2368, 2370, 2371, 2372, 2373, 2374, 2376, 2378, 2382
C1	4-4-2	(2)	4424, 4447
C2	4-4-2	(2)	3984, 3986
C6	4-4-2	(5)	532, 698, 702, 1680, 1792
C7	4-4-2	(20)	706, 716, 717, 719, 728, 737, 2163, 2164, 2166, 2167, 2168, 2169, 2170, 2172, 2195, 2198, 2199, 2204, 2206, 2208
D2	4-4-0	(5)	4180, 4386, 4387, 4390, 4398
D20	4-4-0	(11)	707, 711, 713, 1207, 1232, 1260, 1665, 2018, 2021, 2022, 2101
D49	4-4-0	(8)	232 *The Badsworth*, 235 *The Bedale*, 247 *The Blankney*, 255 *The Braes of Derwent*, 256 *Hertfordshire*, 269 *The Cleveland*, 336 *The Quorn*, 352 *The Meynell*
F8	2-4-2T	(1)	1581
G5	0-4-4T	(1)	381
J21	0-6-0T	(4)	34, 1516, 1807, 1809
J23	0-6-0	(4)	2471, 2472, 2516, 2518
J24	0-6-0	(9)	1821, 1823, 1842, 1844, 1850, 1942, 1951, 1952, 1956
J25	0-6-0	(1)	2060
J26	0-6-0	(5)	412, 525, 554, 818, 1130
J27	0-6-0	(6)	2352, 2353, 2355, 2383, 2386, 2392
J39	0-6-0	(2)	1470, 1487
J71	0-6-0T	(13)	237, 296, 347, 399, 447, 495, 499, 1084, 1134, 1140, 1155, 1167, 1758
J72	0-6-0T	(10)	500, 1746, 2182, 2313, 2319, 2328, 2331, 2332, 2333, 2334
J77	0-6-0T	(8)	138, 290, 999, 1000, 1313, 1346, 1348, 1431
J78	0-6-0CT	(1)	590
K3	2-6-0	(12)	17, 28, 39, 52, 1300, 1312, 1318, 1395, 1396, 1397, 1398
N12	0-6-2T	(1)	2485
Q6	0-8-0	(1)	2228
Q7	0-8-0	(1)	628
X3	2-2-4T	(1)	690

Total 165
Service Stock
Engineer's Yard

Y1	0-4-0T	(1)	45

York Locomotive Allocation 15 March 1943

A1	4-6-2	(5)	2569 *Gladiator*, 2570 *Tranquil*, 2572 *St Gatien*, 2576 *The White Knight*, 2577 *Night Hawk*
A7	4-6-2T	(5)	1126, 1176, 1180, 1183, 1193
B16	4-6-0	(69)	840, 841, 842, 843, 844, 845, 846, 847, 848, 849, 906, 908, 909, 911, 914, 915, 920, 921, 922, 923, 924, 926, 927, 928, 929, 930, 931, 932, 933, 934, 936, 937, 942, 943, 1371, 1372, 1373, 1374, 1375, 1376, 1377, 1378, 1379, 1380, 1381, 1382, 1383, 1384, 1385, 2363, 2364, 2365, 2366, 2367, 2368, 2369, 2370, 2371, 2372, 2373, 2374, 2375, 2376, 2377, 2378, 2379, 2380, 2381, 2382
C1	4-4-2	(2)	4424, 4447
C7	4-4-2	(10)	706, 717, 719, 720, 728, 732, 737, 2163, 2164, 2166
D20	4-4-0	(4)	708, 725, 1260, 2027
D49	4-4-0	(13)	205 *The Albrighton*, 222 *The Berkeley*, 226 *The Bilsdale*, 235 *The Bedale*, 255 *The Braes of Derwent*, 258 *The Cattistock*, 274 *The Craven*, 279 *The Cotswold*, 288 *The Percy*, 298 *The Pytchley*, 352 *The Meynell*, 353 *The Derwent*, 359 *The Fitzwilliam*
J21	0-6-0	(13)	300, 470, 778, 806, 871, 965, 997, 1315, 1514, 1555, 1573, 1596, 1615
J71	0-6-0T	(14)	165, 237, 239, 449, 482, 495, 972, 1085, 1134, 1140, 1167, 1196, 1836
J72	0-6-0T	(11)	500, 1728, 1746, 2178, 2182, 2308, 2315, 2319, 2328, 2332, 2334
J77	0-6-0T	(9)	138, 290, 998, 1000, 1313, 1346, 1348, 1349, 1431
V2	2-6-2	(20)	3643, 3648, 3656, 3660, 3661, 3666, 3672, 3673, 3674, 4808 *The Green Howards*, 4809 *Alexandra, Princess of Wales's Own Yorkshire Regiment*, 4810, 4814, 4818 *St Peter's School, York, AD 627*, 4827, 4835, 4872, 4875, 4878, 4889, 4896
Y8	0-4-0T	(1)	559
D(SR)	4-4-4	(2)	Southern Railway 2051, 2068

Total 178

Service Stock

Engineer's Yard

Y1	0-4-0T	(1)	45

York Locomotive Allocation 2 October 1954

A1	4-6-2	(5)	60121 *Silurian*, 60138 *Boswell*, 60140 *Balmoral*, 61046 *Peregrine*, 60153 *Flamboyant*
A2/2	4-6-2	(3)	60501 *Cock o'the North*, 60502 *Earl Marischal*, 60503 *Lord President*
A2/3	4-6-2-	(4)	60512 *Steady Aim*, 60515 *Sun Stream*, 60522 *Straight Deal*, 60524 *Herringbone*
A2	4-6-2	(1)	60526 *Sugar Palm*
B1	4-6-0	(15)	61002 *Impala*, 61015 *Duiker*, 61016 *Inyala*, 61020 *Gemsbok*, 61038 *Blacktail*, 61053, 61071, 61084, 61115, 61176, 61224, 61288, 61337, 61338, 61339
B16	4-6-0	(46)	61416, 61417, 61418, 61419, 61420, 61421, 61423, 61424, 61426, 61430, 61434, 61435, 61436, 61437, 61438, 61439, 61441, 61443, 61444, 61448, 61449, 61450, 61451, 61452, 61453, 61454, 61455, 61456, 61457, 61458, 61459, 61460, 61461, 61462, 61463, 61464, 61465, 61466, 61467, 61468, 61472, 61473, 61474, 61475, 61476, 61477
D20	4-4-0	(2)	62343, 62345
D49	4-4-0	(7)	62702 *Oxfordshire*, 62730 *Berkshire*, 62731 *Selkirkshire*, 62745 *The Hurworth*, 62759 *The Craven*, 62760 *The Cotswold*, 62774 *The Staintondale*

J25	0-6-0	(6)	65650, 65654, 65677, 65687, 65691, 65700
J27	0-6-0	(10)	65827, 65844, 65845, 65848, 65849, 65874, 65883, 65887, 65890, 65894
J71	0-6-0T	(10)	68230, 68240, 68246, 68250, 68253, 68275, 68280, 68293, 68297, 68313
J72	0-6-0T	(10)	68677, 68695, 68699, 68722, 68724, 68726, 68735, 68739, 68745, 69020
J77	0-6-0T	(1)	68435
J94	0-6-0T	(9)	68029, 68031, 68032, 68040, 68042, 68044, 68046, 68051, 68061
V2	2-6-2	(30)	60837, 60839, 60843, 60847 *St Peter's School, York, AD 627*, 60856, 60864, 60895, 60901, 60904, 60907, 60918, 60925, 60929, 60934, 60941, 60946, 60954, 60960, 60961, 60962, 60963, 60968, 60974, 60975, 60976, 60977, 60978, 60979, 60981, 60982
WD	2-8-0	(10)	90044, 90047, 90056, 90100, 90200, 90424, 90500, 90517, 90518, 90603

Total 169

Service Stock

Motive Power Depot

Y8	0-4-0T	(1)	55

Engineer's Yard

Y1	0-4-0T	(1)	53

York Locomotive Allocation 11 January 1964

Steam

4MT	2-6-0	(4)	43055, 43071, 43097, 43126
A1	4-6-2	(13)	60120 *Kittiwake*, 60121 *Silurian*, 60124 *Kenilworth*, 60126 *Sir Vincent Raven*, 60138 *Boswell*, 60140 *Balmoral*, 60141 *Abbotsford*, 60143 *Sir Walter Scott*, 60145 *Saint Mungo*, 60146 *Peregrine*, 60147 *North Eastern*, 60150 *Willbrook*, 60155 *Borderer*
B1	4-6-0	(11)	61002 *Impala*, 61018 *Gnu*, 61021 *Reitbok*, 61031 *Reedbuck,* 61049, 61062, 61084, 61198, 61275, 61276, 61337
B16	4-6-0	(5)	61421, 61434, 61448, 61454, 61457
J27	0-6-0	(2)	65844, 65894
K1	2-6-0	(18)	62005, 62007, 62009, 62010, 62028, 62029, 62042, 62046, 62047, 62049, 62056, 62057, 62058, 62060, 62061, 62062, 62063, 62065
V2	2-6-2	(26)	60810, 60828, 60831, 60833, 60837, 60847 *St Peter's School, York, AD 627*, 60855, 60856, 60864, 60876, 60877, 60886, 60887, 60895, 60925, 60929, 60932, 60939, 60941, 60942, 60945, 60961, 60963, 60967, 60975, 60982
WD	2-8-0	(7)	90030, 90045, 90078, 90217, 90517, 90518, 90663
9F	2-10-0	(8)	92005, 92006, 92205, 92206, 92011, 92021, 92031, 92039

Diesel

20/3	1Co-Co1	(33)	D252, D253, D254, D258, D259, D275, D276, D278, D281, D282, D283, D284, D285, D345, D346, D347, D348, D349, D350, D351, D352, D353, D354, D355, D356, D357, D385, D386, D387, D388, D389, D390, D391
2/1	0-6-0	(15)	D2046, D2051, D2062, D2063, D2065, D2066, D2075, D2111, D2112, D2113, D2151, D2158, D2159, D2160, D2161
2/13	0-6-0	(4)	D2245, D2268, D2269, D2270
3/1	0-6-0	(15)	D3070, D3071, D3076, D3237, D3238, D3239, D3240, D3313, D3314, D3315, D3319, D3320, D3872, D3874, D3946
11/A1	Bo-Bo	(4)	D5096, D5098, D5099, D5100
12/1	Bo-Bo	(1)	D5176

Total 166

York Locomotive Allocation 1 January 1971

40	(17)	250, 251, 252, 253, 254, 256, 257, 258, 259, 272, 274, 275, 276, 277, 278, 279, 281
47	(18)	1100, 1107, 1513, 1514, 1515, 1516, 1517, 1518, 1519, 1533, 1541, 1542, 1543, 1570, 1571, 1572, 1573, 1574
03	(7)	2054, 2063, 2073, 2075, 2101, 2113, 2150
08	(11)	3076, 3237, 3238, 3239, 3240, 3315, 3319, 3726, 3872, 3874, 4044
20	(11)	8024, 8300, 8301, 8302, 8303, 8304, 8305, 8306, 8307, 8308, 8309

Total 64

York Locomotive Allocation 3 January 1982

The 37 locomotives transferred away when York shed closed on this date were:

To Tinsley
Nos 31141/171/218/220/222/272/327 (7)
To Immingham
Nos 31142/162/168/175/186/188/196/402/403/404/405/406/407/408/409/411 (16)
To Gateshead
Nos 47423/425/426/428/429/430/431/457/458/520/525/526/527/528 (14)

Appendix 4
Significant Rail Accidents in and around York

Fortunately, York has not witnessed a major rail disaster comparable with the likes of Quintinshill (1915), Harrow & Wealdstone (1952) or Clapham (1988). Possibly the 1892 collision at Manor House (north of Thirsk), and the tragic circumstances surrounding the unfortunate signalman James Holmes, is the most significant and widely remembered accident to occur within the immediate locality.

During the early hours of 2 November 1892, an overnight up express from Edinburgh to King's Cross ran into the rear of a stationary freight train at the then Manor House cabin situated some three miles north of Thirsk resulting in 10 fatalities and numerous injuries. Signalman Holmes was held responsible for this disaster due to having fallen asleep and subsequently accepting a train when he already had one in the section. However, in mitigation, he had been up and about all day instead of resting prior to taking duty for a 12hr shift, having to search for a doctor to attend his sick child and when eventually he returned home the child had died. Although not fit for a long night shift on a busy main line, Holmes went to work as no relief was forthcoming, with the almost inevitable result that tiredness and exhaustion would eventually get the better of him — which it did.

Almost two years later, a serious rear-end collision occurred at Castle Hills (just north of Northallerton) on 4 October 1894. This time a freight train was being shunted back into the up relief siding at Castle Hills when it was run into by a double-headed overnight Edinburgh-King's Cross express causing a spectacular amount of damage but only one fatality. This accident was attributed to an alleged misunderstanding between the two drivers as to which of them was responsible for the observance of signals!

At York itself, numerous accidents occurred over the years, luckily without too disastrous consequences. To quote a few examples; on 7 September 1889 a L&Y terminating train ran into the buffers of Platform 6 resulting in 13 injuries — none serious. Then at 9.13am on 27 June 1896 another L&Y train (this time a Todmorden-Scarborough excursion composed of 16 coaches!) was waiting clearance of Waterworks Down Scarborough line advance signal when it was run into by one of the station pilots with eight coaches and two vans attached, due to a misunderstanding between shunters and signalmen. Some injuries were encountered, but fortunately none serious.

Another bay platform buffer stops impact took place at 5.52pm on 18 March 1910 involving a Midland train arriving at Platform 7, again with only slight injuries incurred. A Midland train also got into trouble during a snowstorm at 9.54pm on 18 March 1915 when it was derailed on the junction at Chaloner Whin in the 'moveable switches' (ie: switch diamonds) where the Up Normanton and Down Doncaster lines crossed each other.

A more serious kind of accident occurred on 19 August 1919 when the 9.38pm York-Newcastle and 7.15pm Newcastle-York expresses were in collision at Clifton.

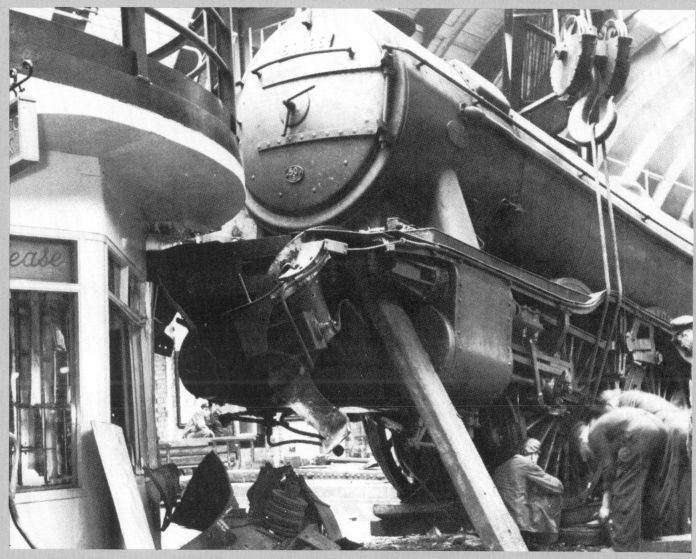

Above:
Class A3 No 60036 *Colombo* **after the buffer stop collision at York (Platform No 12) on 4 August 1958.**
K. Hoole Collection

Above right:
On 31 July 1967 the prototype DP2 collided with a derailed cement wagon. The train involved was the 12.00 King's Cross-Edinburgh service, and the location was south of Thirsk. DP2 was withdrawn as a result of the accident.
J. M. Boyes

Right:
Proof that modern buck-eye-fitted rolling stock can withstand derailments. The 13.00 King's Cross-Edinburgh at Northallerton on 28 August 1979 .
J. M. Boyes

The up train was crossing the path of the down train to gain access to the Up Station Line thence to Platform 14, and the driver of the train on the Down Main had passed signals at danger. The Inspecting Officer, Major G. L. Hall, commented most unfavourably upon the reduced overlap available from Clifton box Down Main home signal — in this case only 25yd.

The derailment of a passenger train entering Platform 8 (13) on 31 March 1920, involving Compound 4-4-0 locomotive No 1619, gave rise to criticism of the facing point wedges then in use, and the subsequent derailment of the 10.35pm Leeds-York train at 11.12pm on 1 June 1922 which took the wrong side of some facing points worked by Locomotive Yard box provoked a recommendation from Major Hall that wedges be replaced by plungers forthwith.

A misunderstanding between shunters and signalmen gave rise to a mishap at 4.5pm on Sunday 30 August 1931 when a light engine enroute from the MPD to the south end of the station collided heavily with a LMS coach conveying a theatrical party from Rhyl to Scarborough resulting in serious injury to one of the dancers.

Another prewar accident happened at 12.52pm on 12 July 1938 involving the coaches of a Newcastle-Scarborough excursion which were stationary on Platform 4 South (now No 3) with brakes applied. The engine backing on to the coaches at the north end to work forward to Scarborough made an extremely heavy impact and several passengers suffered minor injuries and/or shock. Brake failure on 'K3' No 2767 was suspected but never proved. Probably the most spectacular accident to take place at York station occurred on 4 August 1958 when 'A3' Pacific No 60036 *Colombo* working the 9.26am arrival from Sunderland entered No 12 bay platform at speed, mounted the buffer stops and came to rest with the front of the engine up in the air almost touching the footbridge steps. In this case, despite having received correct signal indications for Platform 12, the driver apparently misjudged his braking technique. The front bogie was torn off completely, and luckily again injuries were slight. On 15 June 1965, a collision happened at Waterworks Crossing when a propelled ECS movement from Platform 3 (8) to Clifton Carriage Sidings struck the leading car of an arriving DMU from Scarborough which was proceeding across to Platform 10 (15). In this case, the unsighted driver of the propelled empty stock had gone past some ground position light signals (GPLs) at danger, but

fortunately the DMU driver saw what was likely to happen and braked hard, thus what could have been a nasty accident was averted. Arising out of a recommendation made by the Inspecting Officer, special instructions were published to the effect that such propelling movements must not be allowed to commence until the whole of the intended route throughout has been cleared. Quite a serious accident occurred at 02.48 on Saturday 11 January 1975 when 1S77 23.15 (previous night) King's Cross-Aberdeen car-sleeper not booked to call at York and travelling through the station on the Down Main struck the rear two coaches of 1E40 19.20 (previous night) Aberdeen-King's Cross which was running into the north end of Platform 5 (9). Major G. B. King, whilst holding the driver of 1S77 responsible for passing a signal at danger commented upon the restricted overlap in this particular instance and recommended that delayed clearance control be enforced on the signal immediately preceding that which had been passed at danger. Once more, injuries were relatively light as the impact took place at a low speed.

Away from York, a very serious accident happened south of Thirsk at 15.17 on 31 July 1967. A bulk cement train travelling on the Down Slow line became badly derailed with one wagon foul of the Down Fast line, and almost immediately afterwards the 12.00 King's Cross-Edinburgh hauled by prototype diesel locomotive DP2 — travelling at high speed on a parallel line — ploughed into the wreckage. Seven passengers were killed and 45 injured, 15 of them seriously, and the cause of this very unfortunate accident was attributed to the bad riding characteristics of one of the cement wagons.

What could have been a major disaster occurred at Northallerton on 28 August 1979 involving the complete derailment of 1S79 13.00 King's Cross-Edinburgh. This time good luck prevailed for the derailed HST remained upright with the coaches remarkably well in line, and only one passenger required treatment for shock. The leading pair of wheels under power car No 254028 had become locked causing them to skid, and as they hit a set of points in the Northallerton station area the train became derailed at a speed of around 70mph — the driver having already reduced his speed sensing that something was amiss.

Note:
Readers wishing to learn more about railway accidents, particularly the lessons to be learned from them, are advised to make an appointment to consult the full set of Accident Reports (going back to 1840) which are held by the National Railway Museum Library at York.

Bibliography

The NER: Its Rise and Development; W. W. Tomlinson, 1914

Control on the Railways; P. Burtt, 1926

The Locomotives of Sir Nigel Gresley; O. S. Nock, 1945

The East Coast Route; G. Dow, 1951

A Regional History of the Railways of Great Britain: Volume 4 The North East; K. Hoole, 1965/74/86

The North Eastern Railway; C. J. Allen, 1964/74

The LNER; C. J. Allen, 1966/71

British Railway Signalling; O. S. Nock, 1969

The Derwent Valley Light Railway; S. J. Reading, 1967/76 and 1978* (*Edited by D. S. M. Barrie)

The Easingwold Railway; K. E. Hartley, 1970

The Easingwold Railway; R. N. Redman, 1991

George Hudson of York; A. J. Peacock and D. Joy, 1971

North Eastern Locomotive Sheds; K. Hoole, 1972

Forgotten Railways: North East England; K. Hoole, 1973/1984

The Railways of York; K. Hoole, 1976

The ECML since 1925; K. Hoole, 1977

York 100/1877-1977; S. Rankin and D. Thompson, 1977

Rail Centres: York; K. Hoole, 1983

This is York – The Story of a Station; S. Rankin and D. Thompson, 1984

Railway Stations of the North East; K. Hoole, 1985

Speed on the East Coast Main Line; P. W. B. Semmens, 1990

Electrifying the East Coast Route; P. W. B. Semmens, 1991

The following publications are also of interest: *NER/LNER Magazine; Railway Gazette; Railway Magazine; Modern Railways; Board of Trade* and *Ministry of Transport* records.

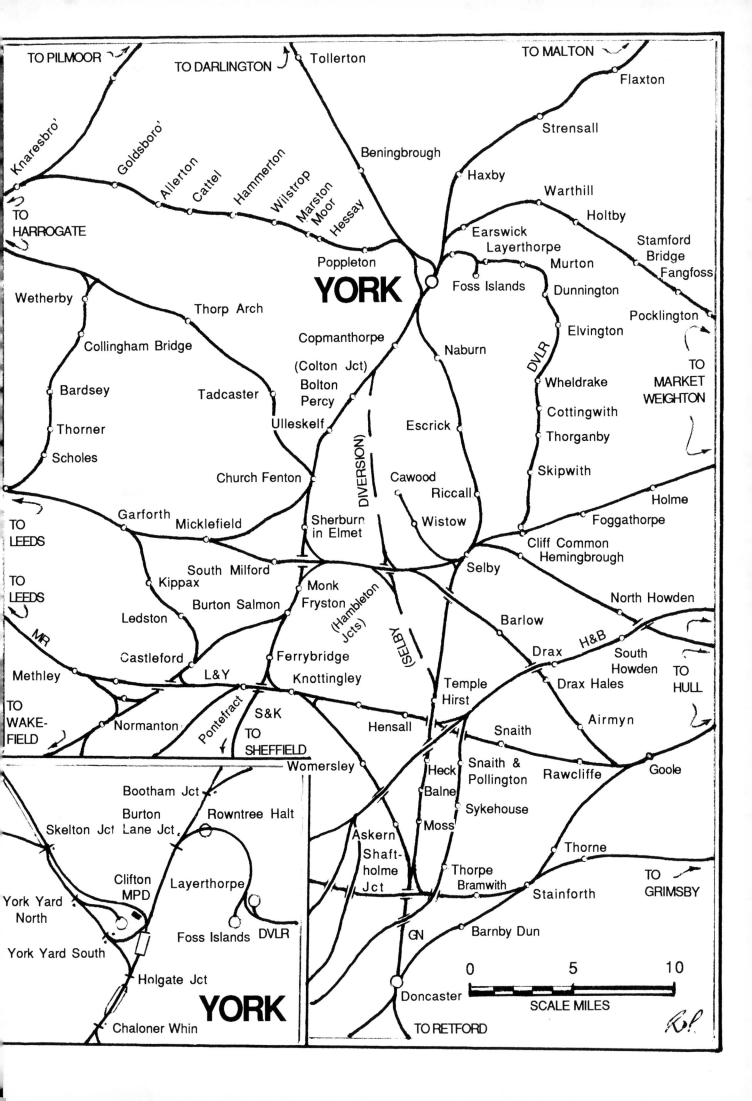